The Only Way is Up

The most important season in Doncaster Rovers' history

A Diary of Events
by
Ian McMahon

Edited by Peter Tuffrey

Doncaster 1999

£9.95

This book is dedicated to Elise, Connor and Nolan.

First published in 1999 by Bond Publications, 8 Wrightson Avenue, Warmsworth, Doncaster, South Yorkshire DN4 9QL.
Tel: 01302 310294.   e-mail: peter@tuffrey.fsnet.co.uk

Printed by Trafford Print (Colour Ltd)
Doncaster

ISBN: 1 872062 03 2

The Only Way is Up
The most important season in Doncaster Rovers' history

Introduction

Before beginning an account of my first year as chief executive of trouble-torn Doncaster Rovers, I suppose some brief details about myself are necessary.

My father was born in Glasgow, but brought up in Ireland. Later, he became a chef and, while he has no sporting connections, his brother once played football as a semi-professional. My mother was born in Yorkshire. I was born in Wells, Somerset in 1964, the youngest of three brothers, though have lived most of my life in the red rose county of Lancashire. Sport has always been a part of my life and it soon became apparent that I had some ability in 'the beautiful game' (football), playing in mid-field.

A number of scouts came knocking on my door and, on leaving school at 16, I joined Oldham Athletic when they were in the old Second Division. I accepted an apprenticeship with them in 1981. However, things did not work out so, following a few first team games, I went on loan to Rochdale, signing for them in January 1984. Things went very well at 'Dale' and I was on the verge of a 'big money' transfer to either a first division (now the Premier League) or a second division side. But, it was not to be. I received an injury in March 1986, at the tender age of 21 and, after complications set in, retired in 1987. I had managed 91 league/cup appearances and scored eight goals.

From 1987, I studied marketing, became a qualified coach and eventually set up as a sports consultant. I have worked mainly within professional sport in various senior positions. I even found time, thanks to funding from the Professional Footballers Association, to gain a Post Graduate Diploma in Business Management.

A picture of myself during the 1984-1985 season at Rochdale F.C.

I've also studied acting, thinking it would be beneficial in a number of ways: helping me cope with public speaking and radio/television interviews. I never had any aspirations of being the next Brad Pitt though, amazingly, I was actually offered two small film roles, one as a detective, the other as a bad guy. Unfortunately, I was unable to take them due to work commitments at the time. What a blow to the entertainment industry. But, who knows, one day, I may return to have another go.

At my desk in Belle Vue (Photo from Sheffield Newspapers).

In 1998, a consortium (Westferry), which was buying Doncaster Rovers Football Club, offered me a job there as chief executive. Initially, I pondered on the sanity of the consortium's members. The team had just been relegated from the Football League, and there was a deep hatred amongst the fans of the existing owners, unlike any ever seen before in football. Managers had come and gone with alarming regularity, attendance figures had plummeted and there were no sponsors. Fans only attended home games to vent their anger on the existing regime. Yet, after a while, the idea appealed to me, and I was keen to accept the challenge, once Westferry had taken control.

Prior to accepting the Doncaster job, I had only been to the town once, and that was many years ago, to see a former football colleague. As a footballer, I never played at Doncaster. When Rochdale met Doncaster Rovers, I didn't play because of an injury.

If readers imagine this book to be about the misery of working at Doncaster Rovers, coupled with tales of cold pies, they will be seriously mistaken. Quite simply, it is about my thoughts and actions, during what was described as the most important season in the long history of Doncaster Rovers Football Club. It also details a year in the life of myself, a former professional footballer who, decided one day, that he needed a challenge. A challenge it certainly was, turning the team, once dubbed 'the worst in professional football,' into winners of the Endsleigh Cup.

Hopefully, the book will give readers an honest account of a club 'fighting for its life' and the occasional chuckle. I do like to do things with a smile on my face.

I would like to thank the following people for their help: Malcolm Billingham, Mike Davies, Shaun Flannery, Paul Gilligan, Ian Green, Dennis Lound, Paul May, Dave Parker, Kevin Phelan, Mike Royston, John Ryan, Glynn Snodin, Ian Snodin, and Peter Tuffrey.

The Only Way is Up

The most important season in Doncaster Rovers' history

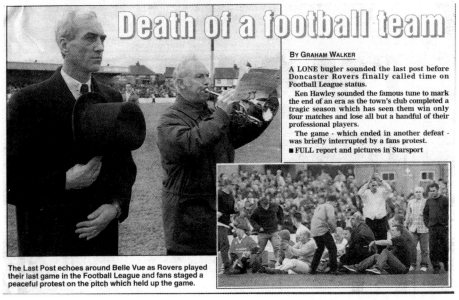

The Last Post echoes around Belle Vue as Rovers played their last game in the Football League and fans staged a peaceful protest on the pitch which held up the game.

The front cover of the Doncaster Star, Monday 4 May 1998.

May 1998

A consortium, looking at buying Doncaster Rovers Football Club, approach me with a job offer. I have met some members of the consortium previously and gather that negotiations surrounding the purchase of the club – just relegated from the Football League, with the worst record in its history – have been going on for some time. Peter Tunks, a colleague and somebody who I have liaised with on many occasions at Oldham rugby league and Hull City/Hull Sharks, introduced me to the consortium. He had mentioned the Doncaster project to me earlier in March, but I never gave it much thought. I had read about the situation there with interest and noted the football team's appalling results and low attendance figures. At that time, I was working as a sports consultant and there were many job opportunities for me to consider, several in America being amongst them. I also said: 'Nobody in their right mind would touch Doncaster Rovers with a barge pole.'

June 1998

The consortium asks if I am interested in 'heading up the Doncaster operation.' So, I have an informal meeting with several representatives in a pub just outside Dewsbury, off the M62. This is the most convenient location for everyone to reach. Before entering the meeting, I note the make of each member's car, trying to gauge the type of people I'm dealing with. Thankfully nobody appears in a Lada. Those in attendance include Paul

The last post
The last game
The last straw

Double pitch invasion completes a season of shame as Rovers drop out of Football League

Rovers go out with the worst ever record

Division Three

	P	W	D	L	F	A	Pts
Notts County	46	29	12	5	82	43	99
Macclesfield	46	23	13	10	63	44	82
Lincoln City........	46	20	15	11	60	51	75
Colchester	46	21	11	14	72	60	74
Torquay..............	46	21	11	14	68	59	74
Scarborough......	46	19	15	12	67	58	72
Barnet................	46	19	13	14	61	51	70
Scunthorpe........	46	19	12	15	56	52	69
Rotherham	46	16	19	11	67	61	67
Peterborough	46	18	13	15	63	51	67
Leyton Orient	46	19	12	15	62	47	66
Mansfield	46	16	17	13	64	55	65
Shrewsbury	46	16	13	17	61	62	61
Chester..............	46	17	10	19	60	61	61
Exeter	46	15	15	16	68	63	60
Cambridge Utd..	46	14	18	14	63	57	60
Hartlepool..........	46	12	23	11	61	53	59
Rochdale	46	17	7	22	56	55	58
Darlington..........	46	14	12	20	56	72	54
Swansea............	46	13	11	22	49	62	50
Cardiff...............	46	9	23	14	48	52	50
Hull	46	11	8	27	56	83	41
Brighton	46	6	17	23	38	66	35
Doncaster	46	4	8	34	30	113	20

Headlines and tables from the Doncaster Star, Monday 4 May 1998

May, Ian Green, Kevin Phelan and myself. I also judge people's characters by the type of shoes they wear. I feel this is a good yardstick. Thankfully, everyone is looking well-heeled. I feel quite relaxed, not really needing the job and insist on 'no bullshit' at the meeting. I want to know what is happening at Doncaster as, during my time in professional sport, I have met many unreliable, whimsical and, it has to be said, untrustworthy people. The consortium's plan is to take over the football and rugby clubs, which are 'both on their arses'.

'Why?' is the obvious question.

They explain their intentions to develop Belle Vue, the site of the football ground, and a proposal of building a new stadium, housing both the football and rugby clubs.

I am very impressed with their plans, and promise to talk to them again in a few days.

Travelling back home along the M62, I consider that my career is going along very nicely and, do I want the Doncaster job compromising it? I decide to decline the offer.

On arriving home, my two boys greet me.

'Can I play out?' asks Connor who, at six-years-old, displays the maturity of someone much older.

'No, I mean, yes. Oh, go and ask your mother.'

My wife, Elise, greets me with the question every husband dreads: 'What would you like for dinner?'

After the last couple of hours, this is not what I wanted to hear. I would have preferred her to say: 'I've done so-and-so for dinner.' This is because, broadly speaking, men are no good at deciding what to eat.

She eventually disappears into the kitchen, saying she will surprise me.

A Rovers fan protests in the centre circle at the home game with Hull City, 4 April, 1998
(Photo by Ray Gilbert)

Protesting Rovers fans gather at the Park Hotel, Carr House Road, in readiness for the short funeral march to Belle Vue on 2 May 1998 (Photo by Ray Gilbert).

Later, whilst tucking into some home-made pasta with pesto sauce, we discuss the Doncaster Rovers job. I state that I like the people who are involved, but think I will turn it down.

'Why?' she asks.

'Well, the team have just been relegated to the Football Conference, and the fans are up in arms at the boardroom antics.'

'Yes, but the new consortium is attempting to put things right, on and off the field, aren't they?'

Of course she is right, and it occurs to me that many husbands must make far-reaching decisions after discussing matters with their wives. The husbands taking all the credit for the success they subsequently achieve.

A couple of days later, I speak to Kevin Phelan who reveals the consortium would like to offer me a job controlling the football and rugby clubs at Doncaster.

I am delighted to accept the offer, is my reply, providing we can work out a suitable deal.

Several conversations and meetings follow, and it is agreed that I carry out some research for the job. Contracts to take over Doncaster Rovers have been exchanged and the completion date is planned for 31 July. Eventually, I learn that the Club does not have a manager, and there is only a handful of full-time professional players, along with a few YTS lads. The FA's community programme, which helps coach kids in schools, is struggling through lack of business funding. No company in the Doncaster area wants to be seen helping the present regime controlling the Club, as they would be regarded as 'scabs', and nobody is going to risk that. Later, I am persuaded that it is better to take over a club without any inherited problems. It's a good job I love a challenge.

Kevin Phelan invites me to Dublin to agree a contract. It is my first visit to Ireland, and I am excited, visiting the land of my forefathers. My father was born in Scotland, but brought up in Clones, County Monaghan. He often spoke of his life in Ireland, before eventually leaving to find fame and fortune (which he never did).

I land in Dublin around 1pm, and immediately sense an affinity with the country. After all, McMahon's have been raised in Ireland for centuries. It is also interesting to note that, had I been selected to play football at international level, I was eligible to represent Ireland, even though I was born in England.

I meet Kevin Phelan and we move on to a pub, ironing-out my contract details over a pint of the 'black stuff.'

I'm back in Manchester by 4.30 pm. Now, that's how to do business!

2 July 1998

Kevin and myself are on our way to meet Ken Richardson and Mark Weaver to discuss details surrounding the completion of the take-over. I'm unsure about what to expect, or the reception we'll get. One thing is for sure, these two are definitely not flavour-of-the-month in Doncaster.

July 1998

It's difficult for an outsider like myself to understand the reasons behind Doncaster Rovers being where they are. Suffice to say, something has to be done, and the sooner the better. Each time that the take-over date is put back, the situation is made worse, being unable to plan pre-season training, friendly matches, recruit a manager and players.

On arrival at Ken Richardson's East Riding Sacks company offices near York, we are met by most of the Doncaster Rovers board, which includes Mark Weaver, Julie Richardson, Ken Harron and Reg Ashworth. During an 'interesting' meeting, we agree to put out a joint press release the following week. The wording is very carefully chosen with each camp fighting their own corner. After the meeting, Kevin drops me off at the Ferrybridge service station, and I 'phone Elise, relaying details about the afternoon.

Driving home, the enormity of the Doncaster Rovers project brings a smile to my face, and I sing along to a tune being played on a radio station. I wonder if people driving past are looking at me and commenting: Isn't that Ian McMahon, the man who will turn Doncaster into a sporting Mecca? On second thoughts, it is more likely they're saying: Look at that bloody idiot there, probably singing along to a Spice Girls' number.

Sunday 5 July

I get up early for a game of golf with my brother, Paul, and friend Chubby, leaving at 5.30 am, to tee-off at 6.15. If you ask me, we must be mad for getting up at this time. I

In action for Rochdale against Northampton, during the 1984/85 season.

tee off into the trees, and wonder what on earth I am doing. All this talk about footballers, even ex-footballers, being natural sportsmen is rubbish. People enquire why I even consider participating in another sport, with my knee being shot to pieces. Surely, just playing golf, will only make it worse, they ask. Well, yes, but we are dead for a long time, and must enjoy life while we can. My professional football career was cut short when I was only 21, but since that time I have had some fun. I played basketball for two seasons, amateur football as a goalie, Sunday football as a very slow centre forward, the team winning a cup. I bet on hearing this last fact, ex-Oldham manager Joe Royle will regret letting me go to Rochdale.

The quality of golf is erratic and our conversation drifts towards Doncaster Rovers.

P.M.: 'Have you taken this job at Donny?'

I.M.: 'Yes, I'm already working on one or two things.'

C.: 'I bet, before long, you'll be asking us to play for them.'

P.M.: 'What do you mean?'

C.: 'Hasn't he told you, they haven't even got any players?'

P.M.: 'Sounds interesting.'

I.M.: 'At least by having no players, we can start from scratch.'

C.: 'You can certainly say that again.'

Our game ends in a draw with me having seven pars, which is not bad considering the way I started.

Later in the day, Elise and I decide to take Connor and Nolan to Cannon Hall, Barnsley, which has a small farm. Nolan tries desperately to join most of the animals in their pens, while Connor, showing that he takes after me, is terrified to go anywhere near them. Eventually, after his mother threatens to ground him for a week, he strokes one of the animals.

While in South Yorkshire, we decide to travel to Doncaster, to look at the Rovers' ground.

'It can't be that bad,' I explain to Elise.

Once we're there, I stare in amazement, mumbling, in my best Victor Meldrew voice: 'I don't believe it, I don't believe it.'

'Where are we?' Connor asks.

'This is where your daddy is going to work,' answers my wife, with a slight hint of sarcasm.

The car park is an unbelievable sight, with deep puddles everywhere. About a dozen advertising hoardings, displayed in an ad-hoc fashion on the front of the stand, conspire to make it an eyesore. We all gaze at the shabby porta-cabins standing adjacent, and I explain these are being used as office accommodation. Offices within the stand were damaged during a major fire in 1995.

'Oh,' comes the astonished reply.

The aftermath of the Belle Vue main stand fire in 1995 (Photo by Shaun Flannery)

We decide to move on, in case I am asked to play for the Doncaster Dragons, who have a game here tonight. Like the football club, the Dragons too have stumbled upon hard times. We take the kids to play at Charlie Chalk's Fun Factory, and then on to a McDonalds' – where else? These are located amidst a large leisure park close to the ground. The kids enjoy themselves, the journey at least having some advantages.

On the way home, Elise expresses her concern about the length of time it will take for me to travel to work every day. The journey, each way today, has taken 1 hour 45 minutes.

'It won't be too bad,' I answer.

By coincidence, during the evening, Channel 5 is showing a documentary about Doncaster Rovers' last few months in the Football League. Supporters are shown carrying a coffin to the last home game. The Club, by this time, had long been relegated to the Conference. Strong views are expressed by the fans and members of a 'Save the Rovers' group.

Nearly everyone interviewed believes the Club is facing extinction. Elise and I are watching together and, during the first commercial break, it is noticeable that she looks ashen.

'Are you alright ?' I ask.

'Are you sure you want to work there? ...Will it be safe?' she retorts.

'What you must understand is, I haven't done anything wrong. So, what have I got to worry about?'

'I suppose you are right,' she concedes, running upstairs to calm our squabbling kids.

I watch the remainder of the programme and conclude that, whilst there is hatred for the regime presently controlling the Club, the consortium I'm working for is not involved with them in any way. And, we know what has to be done ... It all sounds simple enough.

Ian Green, Paul May and myself will involve ourselves in running the Club, while Kevin Phelan will broker the deal.

My friend and golfing partner, Chubby, has obviously been watching the programme too, and he 'phones, taking the mickey out of me for accepting the Doncaster job. He even offers to play for us. Eventually, we have a serious conversation about the situation there and agree that at least the Doncaster fans care about the Club, and that's a good start.

Funeral/protest march to Belle Vue, 2 May 1998, passing along Carr House Road
(Photo by Ray Gilbert).

July 1998

As midnight approaches, I sit in front of my computer, putting an action plan together. Recalling that we have no manager, no players, no coaches, no physio, no training facilities, no sponsors, no kit, and no boots. The songs 'Things can only get better' and 'The only way is up,' come to mind.

Rovers in turmoil

- **No manager**
- **Only four pros**
- **Two weeks to training**

DONCASTER Rovers boss Mark Weaver has admitted he is worried because there is still no manager in place at Belle Vue.

The club is only a couple of weeks away from the time when it would normally be considering pre-season training and still has no football manager in place. And there are only four professional players and a handful of youth teamers on the books.

Weaver admitted: "It's a concern to everyone but, on the other hand, I'm told the club is going to be taken over.

Mark Weaver: worried

By David Kessen

"I don't want to be blamed for putting someone in and it then costing the club more money if new owners don't want him and have to spend money to get rid of him.

"If I had had to put a deadline on getting someone in, I would have put it at about four weeks ago. That would have been the best opportunity. Every week now is a delay.

Serious

"We should be looking at training in two weeks time if we are to be serious challengers but if we started at the moment we would not have enough for five-a-side game. It's got to be a worry for fans and everyone.

"I feel like I'm waiting at the side of the motorway for a lift – I keep saying I'll give it another five minutes before I give up, and that's how it feels with waiting for a takeover to go through."

Weaver has stated he wants to leave recruitment of players for next season to any new manager and no more have been brought in since a clear-out at the end of last season.

The four professionals on the books are Lee Warren, Danny George, Harvey Cunningham and Darren Brookes.

A spokesman for the Irish consortium which has been bidding to buy Rovers said earlier this month that a deal had been struck over the sale of the club.

But current owners Ken Richardson and Dinard Trading are still in control at present.

The club is now out of administration after paying off its debts under a creditors voluntary agreement.

Extract from the Doncaster Star, Wednesday 24 June 1998.

Monday 6 July

I speak with Chris Griffin, financial controller at the Football League, to discover how much money Doncaster Rovers can expect to receive from them for the forthcoming season. He politely informs me that, whilst it would be unusual, the Football League do not have to give us any money. But, the issue will be dealt with at a meeting to be held on 16 July. I agree to send him information regarding the new holding company, the Club's structure and its directors. I will also mention that we are staying 'full-time' for the 1998/1999 season. There will be no part-time players, at least, not in the foreseeable future.

SOLD OFF

Rovers bought by Irish consortium

Headline from the Doncaster Star, Monday 6 July 1998.

I have a similar conversation about the new make up of Doncaster Rovers with Mike Appleby at the Football Association, and agree to send him details. I also speak to Peter Hunter, Chief Executive of the Conference, and he says he will forward our fixture list for the season.

'Can you tell me who our first game is against?' I probe.

'Well, the first Conference matches begin on Saturday 15 August and you play ... Dover Athletic away.'

'Away? You are bloody joking,' I shout down the 'phone.

'Yes, sorry about that one,' he answers.

In spite of this, we end the conversation on friendly terms, and I invite both himself and the Chairman of the Conference to visit Doncaster once Westferry have officially taken over.

The press release, drafted in Ken Richardson's offices, should have been received by a number of sports journalists today. And, I decide to drive to Doncaster, and buy a newspaper, gauging any reaction to the news.

My wife thinks I am mad, saying: 'Get someone to send you a paper.'

'No, I need see one today,' I reply.

Two hours later, on reaching South Yorkshire, I pick up the Doncaster Star, reading: 'Sold off-Rovers bought by Irish consortium.'

'I don't believe it. I don't believe it,' I mouth, switching to my Victor Meldrew voice (again).

July 1998

The newspaper has made a mockery of a simple press release. All the members of the consortium are English, and are based in this country. The consortium has no Irish connections other than with a firm of accountants, based in Dublin – and that information was not disclosed. To cap it all, the fans still believe Ken Richardson is involved with the Club. Absolutely amazing. I suppose I am disappointed because I wanted the Press to focus on the positive aspects of the take-over. This headline seemingly creates more anxiety and mistrust.

Tuesday 7 July

I meet David McKnight, a well-established sports agent. He is involved with the take-over, being brought in by Kevin Phelan, and given the responsibility of trying to find Doncaster Rovers a manager and some players. We discuss a strategy, agreeing that not many people have the opportunity of building up a football club from nothing. We discuss potential candidates for the post of manager, and prepare an advertisement for the position, to be placed in local and national newspapers, at the end of the week. One person whose name has figured prominently for the post is that of Ian Snodin, a former Rovers player himself. He was an England Under-21 international and also played for Leeds United and Everton. He is now at Scarborough, where his brother Glynn, another ex-Rovers player, is the youth team coach. I mention to David that we ought to talk to Ian, discovering if he is interested in becoming Rovers' manager.

The evening is a relatively quiet one, Connor attending Ju-Jitsu classes, while Nolan just amuses himself. I watch the World Cup semi-final between Holland and Brazil, having a feeling that Holland will win. They lose, despite being the best team. My knowledge of world football seems to be lacking.

Wednesday 8 July

I 'phone Ian Snodin, learning he is definitely interested in managing Doncaster Rovers. We arrange to meet – half way between our respective homes – in Brighouse, near Halifax, tomorrow. I also wonder if he can take Doncaster Rovers out of their present gloom and become a local folk hero.

The evening is spent watching the World Cup semi-final between France and Croatia, and working on structures and budgets for the season ahead. I start with a blank piece of paper, and muse that Bill Gates probably started out in a similar way. I decide the proposals will have to be very sketchy until I obtain more information, but at least they will provide a basis on which to go forward.

Whilst France beat Croatia, they have Laurent Blanc sent off. This means he will miss the final and I ponder on how he is feeling. Perhaps he may fancy playing for us against Dover. After all, it is only across the pond. He could also bring us some duty-free booze to sell in the bar. I then realise we don't have a bar. We don't even have any players.

Thursday 9 July

A busy day ahead for me, the chief executive officer designate of Doncaster Rovers. As usual, the day starts with Connor and Nolan running around fighting over various issues.

I subsequently drive my wife to work and drop the kids off at school, using her car until I can sort one out for myself. On returning home, I change and prepare for the meeting with Ian Snodin. But, I am constantly interrupted by numerous 'phone calls.

I realise that time is moving on and quickly shower and shave. Then, disaster. I discover there are no ironed shirts in my wardrobe. I will have to iron one myself. My mind wonders to a picture of Martin Edwards, chairman and chief executive of Manchester United – standing in his boxer shorts, with tissue on his face, having cut himself shaving-ironing a shirt for himself, before an important meeting.

I travel along the M62 to the arranged meeting point with Ian Snodin at Forte Posthouse, Brighouse, West Yorkshire.

The meeting is a success. Ian understands the present situation at Doncaster, and has clear ideas about how players can be attracted to the Club. Without a doubt, I feel he is the right person for the job. He also wants brother Glynn to be his assistant, and feels there is a good chance of him agreeing to the proposal. The prospect of both brothers joining the Club would, I am sure, excite the Doncaster fans. I agree to arrange another meeting, where David McKnight and myself can discuss matters further with him. Hopefully, if Glynn is interested in returning to Doncaster, he will come along too. Whilst Ian is earning more at Scarborough than we can afford to pay, we discuss a 'package', and I feel sure a bonus structure can be agreed. After all, we are trying to get back into the Football League at the first attempt and will be happy to relate pay to performance.

Later, I drive to the head offices of the Professional Footballers' Association in Manchester, meeting Roger Reade who is in charge of the Football in the Community Scheme. This enables clubs to coach in schools and promote themselves. The scheme at Doncaster Rovers, like everything else there, has encountered problems. I discover that Roger is a former Doncaster Rovers' secretary, and used to have shares in the Club. He still lives in Doncaster, and we discuss Rovers at length, during which time he gives me some indication of how the fans feel. I consider telling him about my talk with Ian Snodin, only decide against it. By coincidence, he actually states that Ian or Glynn would be the fans' favourites to join the Club. Little does he know that, by this time next week, they both could be appointed.

From there, I move on to see Mick McGuire, assistant chief executive of the P.F.A. He has dealt with Doncaster Rovers for two years, and we discuss the past and present situations at the Club. We also talk about a problem concerning Robert Betts, one of our schoolboys, who played for Rovers first team last season, but has since signed for Coventry City.

Robert Betts (left) playing for Rovers against Colchester 2 May 1998
(Photo by Paul Gilligan).

Later, debating the same issue with Kevin Phelan, he says he will get hold of Ken Richardson and Mark Weaver and find out what is going on, as we may be able to claim some compensation.

During the evening, I 'phone Ian Snodin, making arrangements to speak to club officials at Scarborough. I agree to talk with him again tomorrow, and will contact Mick Wadsworth, the Scarborough manager, over the weekend.

Friday 10 July 1998

Phone call from Ian Snodin who has taken the 'phone number of Richard Liburd. He's been recommended by Mick McGuire. I arrange to meet Ian at 10.00 am Tuesday. He tells me that his brother Glynn will probably join Barnsley as reserve team manager, working under John Hendrie, the new first team manager. Shit! What will we do now?

On reaching home, Connor greets me with his school report. It's brilliant. He must get his brains from his mother. I feel very proud of him and hope, one day, he becomes an academic.

Saturday 11 July

During the evening, I'm a DJ at a fund-raising BBQ event held at Connor's school, Woodhouses. It's a little like an Ibiza party night. Well, almost. I play the music of Bewitched, the Spice Girls, and Abba-for all the mums. As might have been predicted – it's a late night. I love listening to music, above anything else. The long journeys to Doncaster, over the coming year, will provide ample opportunities to do this, so I will have to update my CD collection.

Sunday 12 July

I get up at 9.30 am – Nolan rises at 10.00 am, Connor 10.55 am. I read the Sunday papers, learning Dwight Yorke has been offered to Manchester United for £15 million. I pick up a copy of *Yorkshire Sport* to read comments about Doncaster Rovers, gleaned from their recent AGM, and they're not good.

Although it's raining, we decide to shop in Meadowhall, Sheffield where it's very busy, having difficulty finding a parking space. We buy Connor a waterproof watch as a reward for his good school report, together with shin pads, and astro-turf boots for his forthcoming spell in a soccer camp at Oldham Athletic. It seems that these camps are the norm now and, if kids enjoy them, who can criticise? I tell him that I used to play for Oldham, though he seems unimpressed. For most kids, anybody below David Beckham's standard is insignificant.

Schumacher wins British Grand Prix. No surprise there.

In the World Cup Final, there's speculation about whether Ronaldo is playing or not. At half-time France lead 2-0 through two Zidane headers from corner kicks. Jacquet, the French coach, is retiring after the Final. I wonder what chance there would be of him coming to Doncaster to help out? Connor watches the Final with me and, who knows, one day he may play in it.

Denilson makes an impact late on, but wouldn't you expect that from somebody recently sold to Spanish club Celta Vigo for £20m. French defender Desailly is sent off for a second 'bookable' offence with 20 minutes to go, but his team win 3-0. This brings no excitement in the McMahon household.

There was a President McMahon of France in the 17th or 18th century. We are supposed to be related, though it seems questionable. However, Connor can count to ten in French and I passed my French O-Level a year early at school …

Monday 13 July

Another rainy day, but I'm prepared for the events ahead.

I discuss the offer to Ian Snodin with Paul May, a director in the new Doncaster Rovers. He will control all financial matters.

David Beckham arrives back in this country from USA, where he has been spending time with 'Posh' Spice. Since his sending off in the World Cup, some morons have been hounding his family. People ought to realise that football is only a game. Hate campaigns will only drive players, like Beckham, abroad, where Italian and Spanish clubs would obviously welcome a quality player like him.

After a few conversations with Paul May, I am able to devise some realistic financial proposals, spending the evening working on these.

July 1998

Tuesday 14 July

It's amazing how the M62 can sometimes transform itself into a giant car park which, by comparison, makes its southern counterpart, the M25, appear to be free-flowing. A number of 'reps' flash past, with mobile phones permanently attached to their ears, and jackets neatly hanging in the back of their cars. They zig-zag from lane to lane, in the faint hope of inching forward a few seconds ahead of their tight schedules. I arrive at the Forte Posthouse to find the car park is full. Perhaps it's becoming synonymous with clandestine meetings for a variety of purposes. I wander into the lounge area, when a mobile phone rings. It appears as if everybody in the room simultaneously reaches into their jackets or handbags. Also, at the same time, nearly everyone mumbles to themselves, no it's not mine. I'm reminded of the previous Saturday when, against my better judgement, I bought a mobile – once regarded as a 'yuppie' toy. In line with my appointment as chief executive of Doncaster Rovers, all calls regarding the Club can now be made to this, instead of McMahon Towers. The gadget is incredible and such an extravagance for me and Doncaster Rovers. Of course, I don't know how it works and have to rely on Connor to show me.

David McKnight appears and we discuss our tactics for the impending arrival of Ian Snodin – the future manager of Doncaster Rovers – we hope. We are also still hoping that Glynn will be his assistant. In time, Ian Snodin confirms Glynn has been approached to become Barnsley's reserve team manager – missing out on the opportunity of a lifetime, if he doesn't return to Donny Rovers. We order some coffee, and discuss Ian's thoughts and his dreams of taking Rovers back into the Football League. He talks about bringing in another coach, if Glynn is not available. Several times we skirt the financial issues before tackling them. Footballers' contract negotiations are interesting to say the least, and the present situation dredges up some of my own experiences. After failing to impress manager Joe Royle at Oldham Athletic – I wanted to play in mid-field, he said I was a centre-half – I was 'made available.' But, it was not the end of the world – just ask David Platt, Lee Dixon and scores of other players who were advised they were surplus to requirements. And, to be honest, I was delighted to leave. It has also been proved that one manager's free transfer can sometimes be another's star signing.

I arrived at Rochdale, on loan, having been found by Bill Urmson, Oldham Athletic's legendary youth team coach while playing snooker at a local club. If I had practiced 'tactics' as much as I had worked on my snooker action, who knows what I might have achieved. Having dropped down a couple of divisions, by agreeing to go to Rochdale on loan, I thought it was all rather easy until I was sent off in my second game. On my return, I played rather well against Swindon. After the game, I was summoned to manager Jimmy Greenhoff's room. This meant one of two things: a bollocking, or a double bollocking. Very rarely do managers praise players. But, on that day, it was different. Rochdale wanted to sign me on a permanent basis and discuss terms. I asked for five times my 'Oldham' salary. This was in the days before agents acted on behalf of players.

Player/manager Ian Snodin in action (Photo by Shaun Flannery).

'No chance,' said J. Greenhoff. 'But I'll see what I can do.'

That night, someone from Rochdale contacted me at my girlfriend Elise's home – she's now my wife – and I agreed a two-year deal. How easy negotiations seemed to be before agents came into the game.

However, back to the present and the meeting with Ian Snodin. We agree a very ordinary salary, with a good bonus for promotion to the League. David and myself believe Ian will go far. He has a good understanding of football/the situation at Doncaster, and his terms fall within our pay structure. We agree to 'let him know' of our decision in due course. It was an old cliche when, in reality, after he'd gone, we both agree we'd done well to get him. He is, no doubt, driving home thinking the same. I say, I will speak to Mick Wadsworth, the Scarborough manager, for official permission to speak to Ian. Although I know we've done things the wrong way round, circumstances dictate that we cannot afford to hang around.

Mick Wadsworth gives his permission, and it is worth noting that he is, without doubt, one of the best coaches in the country, and should go far.

With the business concluded, I travel back home, over the Pennines, past sheep oblivious to their impending destiny with mint sauce. At home, I speak to Paul May, and he agrees verbally to the Snodin deal. We will finalise everything the following day at the Northampton board meeting.

Later, I receive a surprise call from Florida. Earlier in the year I was offered an opportunity to work out there on a consultancy basis but, unfortunately, due to work commitments, I had to decline. Now, a full-time opportunity has arisen and those concerned wonder if I am interested. With the temperature there, averaging 75 degrees all the year round, you bet I am interested. I agree to discuss the matter further, at a later date, just in case the Donny job doesn't work out. My wife-life's greatest worrier-says 'whatever' when I ask for her opinion on the proposal.

Today, is David Beckham's first day back at training with Manchester United – not Doncaster Rovers – unfortunately.

Wednesday 15 July

The day begins at David McKnight's headquarters, where a call comes from Ian Snodin. He has been thinking about our job offer and, after realising the task ahead, has decided that he needs a two-year contract. To be fair, this is not an unreasonable request, and I agree to discuss it, later in the day, at the board meeting in Paul May's Northampton offices. Eventually, David McKnight, Peter Tunks and myself head along the M6. Peter Tunks, is currently working with David, and both of them are to liaise on the rugby side of the operation. We discuss sport in general, the future of Doncaster Rovers and swap stories from our various sporting careers. Peter Tunks, an Australian rugby league player, has worked in England as a player, coach and administrator. At 6ft 3ins and weighing around 18 stone, he immediately holds our attention, telling us tales of his wilder younger days, when he was more athletic, and about his appearances for Australia.

July 1998

The board meeting and strategies discussed, we travel back north, stopping on the way at a service station for what turns out to be, a very expensive burger. As they serve quorn burgers, I forgive them.

Thursday 16 July

Today, I will approach Scarborough F.C. about Ian Snodin, and discuss a transfer fee/compensation.

I am studying for a Masters Degree in Sport Law, and ponder on the logic of compensation, wondering why footballers and other sports people are the only employees who move from job to job for a transfer fee. How many hairdressers, electricians or even chief executives follow this practice? All they do is give their employer the required notice and move on. Whilst these may be strange comparisons, the principles are the same.

The Bosman ruling now allows free movement in Europe for a footballer over the age of 24, and when they are out of contract. Mark my words, it will not be long before there is free movement of players, at any age, at the end of their contracts. Also, I predict, there will be provisions for 'getting out' of the 'long term' contracts, which are currently being offered to players. The transfer system is outdated and should be abolished, with players being allowed the same freedom of movement between employers as that enjoyed by people in other professions.

Scarborough's Mick Wadsworth remembers me from a coaching course we both attended. He still insists on compensation for Ian Snodin, and the matter is to be dealt with by the chairman Ken Ferrie.

Whilst Mick does not give a figure, he quotes the £20,000 plus incentives (totalling £35k) they had allegedly recently received from Darlington for Gary Bennett, who was a similar age to Ian Snodin. But, Ian Snodin is the club's captain and a very valuable asset (particularly as I have learned that the club is up for sale). Of course I tell Mick that Doncaster has no money to spend on players or managers and, if they insisted on compensation, it would seriously jeopardise the deal. I agree to ring him again tomorrow. In reality, I would pay up to £10,000, but have failed to mention that.

During the evening, I meet Ian Snodin (pronounced Snowdin because Ian's daughter tells me her dad believes Snod-in sounds common). He had a very successful playing career, the highlight being an £840,000 move from Leeds United to Everton, where he spent several years.

Earlier in the day, I received a fax from Mark Weaver, Doncaster Rovers' present general manager, who highlighted the urgent items we need to sort out before 1st August. The list brings a smile to both Ian and myself, and underlines the task ahead. We look at some of the items, in the order they appear on the fax, making the following comments:

Matchday programme: I'll deal with this one when we take-over the Club. At the moment, we don't even have a team, so it will be low on our list of priorities.

Players' bonus structure: We don't have to worry about this yet, having only five professionals and several YTS lads on the books.

Team kit: No we don't have a kit to play in. Probably every Sunday league club has one

23

or even two, but not Doncaster Rovers. We both agree to contact anyone in the sportswear business who has ever spoken to us in the past. I imagine saying to someone: 'Hello, this is Ian McMahon. You may not remember me, but we met once in Tesco in 1982. Will you sponsor Doncaster's kit?'

I even anticipate the reply: 'Doncaster Rovers, the team that's been relegated to the Conference league? The club whose fans refused to attend home games, and where the ground is falling down or, at least, appears to be? ... Of course we will sponsor Doncaster Rovers ...'

Physiotherapist: He has left to join Peterborough United, so we need a new one.

Club doctors: We'll worry about this at a later date.

Training kit: Again we agree to use our contacts, or players will have to bring their own.

Team coach: Whilst most people will expect us to arrive in our cars, I have already arranged a meeting with the MD of coach operators Wallace Arnold for next week. Naturally, I will expect him to give us the coach free-of-charge.

I feel the next few months will include building up a network of contacts in both the public and private sector.

Scene at the last match of the 1997-1998 season (Photo by Paul Gilligan).

Organising a team to play in pre-season friendlies: We agree to cancel all friendlies until after 1st August, the date when we expect to be physically in control of the Club and able to organise our own. Further, by that time, we may have 11 players. I even consider cleaning my boots and making myself available, but maybe I'm not as fit as I used to be. And, I would need an outsize pair of shorts, as I do not look as good in my kit as I used to.

Ground safety certificate: I will deal with this one, as we are supposed to have a good relationship with the local council. I'm anxious that I cannot do anything until we are in control of the day-to-day running of the Club. Every ground has to have a safety certificate, legislation being very tight after the Hillsborough and Bradford disasters. Let us hope that, over years, the present owners have kept things in order, limiting the cost, to ourselves, on remedial work.

Medical kit: There is nothing, and we consider putting a clause into all new players' contracts, asking them to provide their own Elastoplasts and bandages.

Footballs: Unbelievably, Doncaster Rovers do not have any footballs. No wonder they were relegated.

Training facilities: Well, if the Club doesn't have any footballs, or kit, what use are training facilities? Nevertheless, Ian says he will use his contacts, particularly at the town's School for the Deaf, which has the best facilities in the area.

The time approaches 10.30 pm, and we decide to call it a day. Both of us part with smiles on our faces. After all, the one thing we're going to need is a good sense of humour. As we're both married, we've probably got one already.

Driving home, I cannot help but worry over the present situation at the Club. We don't even have enough players for a five-a-side training session, which is fortunate as there are no balls, goal posts, or training facilities. Heaven help us if a player gets injured.

I love a challenge.

Friday 17th July

I make my way to the posh part of sunny Cheshire and David McKnight's Premier Crew offices. I also ring chairman Ken Ferrie at Scarborough, to learn how much compensation they want for Ian Snodin, realising they'll not let him go for nothing. In time, I gather they're asking £3,000, which is very reasonable, though I say I will have to come back to them. They need an answer by 4.30 pm.

Whilst working with David McKnight, I watch a video of a Bulgarian international who is seeking an English club. At £2-£3 m he's maybe a little expensive, but these days, who knows? No, he probably will not be joining Doncaster Rovers. In any event, his wages would be more than the Club's annual turnover. I think back to my first encounter with a foreign player when, as a schoolboy, I watched Oldham's Ricard Kowenicki from Poland. Twelve months later, he and I played together, several times, in Oldham's reserve team. Personally, I do believe that overseas players can enhance football in this country. Yet, having said that, there have been some very average foreigners, paid higher wages than their UK counterparts, and mostly because they have an accent.

During the day, I contact Chas Walker, chairman of the Doncaster Rovers supporters club. Of course he knows that I am connected with the Club – there are seemingly no secrets in football – and is pleased that I have 'phoned. We discuss the way forward and I am always amazed at the amount of information supporters require from a club. C. Walker wants to know where the money is coming from, who the directors are, and what they do?

Wait a minute, I think to myself. You cannot ask those sort of questions. The identity of the directors is not a problem, as they will be announced shortly. But, with the greatest of respect, it's none of your business who the investors are. Rightly, there should be no hidden agendas, though some investors wish to remain anonymous. We have a good chat, both understanding and respecting each other's positions. I agree to meet a couple of members next week and go through the plans for the season ahead, and how we can work together to achieve success.

At 3.55 pm, I 'phone Scarborough F.C., confirming our acceptance of the £3,000 transfer fee for Ian Snodin. We agree to complete the paperwork on Monday.

It's the end of the summer term for my eldest son Connor (six years old), and he's jumping for joy, as I pick him up from school. Already he's switched on to his 'Dad can I have' mode, while I'm adopting a 'no' routine. During the summer holidays, soccer and basketball camps await the young McMahon as he steps out on to a sporting path. Should I tell him now what the pitfalls are, or should I let him find out for himself? I am not a pushy parent and, even if I tried to be one, he would not accept it. Like most children today, he tends to get his own way. And, while he's only six, the garden shed, and indeed, the garden itself, are both littered with sporting equipment for him to use.

New rules currently allow children from around eight-years-old to be 'signed' by a professional team to play and train with their schools of excellence. How many of these children will feel despair when they are rejected only a short time afterwards? Whilst, in theory, it might seem beneficial to encourage children at an early age, it can also have an adverse effect. Connor does not mind which sport he participates in. The only thing I ask of him is to enjoy it and give 100% commitment each time he participates. Already, he swims on Saturday mornings and is an orange belt at Ju-Jitsu-two sports which he was introduced to through friends. Indeed, he began Ju-Jitsu at just four-years-old. Even at this tender age, he has a 'college fund' in place, ready to help him through university. Are these the first signs of a pushy parent? At the moment, his favourite sport is golf, and maybe he is just a little too young for lessons. After watching the English Open at Royal Birkdale who can tell? Let us not forget that Tiger Woods was, himself, a top golfer, at even six-years-old.

Later, after watching more of the Open, I decide I've picked up enough tips for my own game and ring my old chum 'Chubby' to see if he wants a game.

We tee off at 7.00 pm, and I put all thoughts of Doncaster Rovers behind me. In time, I easily win the game, finishing the 18th hole at 10.15 pm.

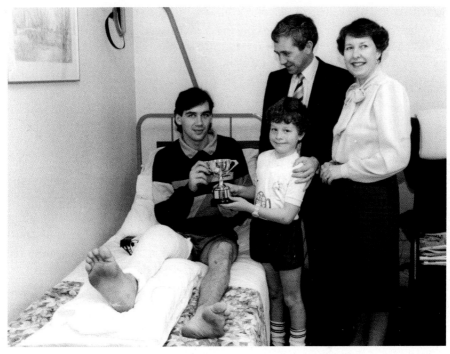

Although injured, I receive the Rochdale F.C. Young Player of the Year award during the 1985-1986 season. I wish I was as thin as this again!

The pressure of working full-time has now curtailed all my sporting exploits, except for the occasional round of golf. I suppose there is a part of me that will forever ask questions about my own football career: How good was I, and how good could I have been? It was unfortunate that my career ended almost before it was under way. I would have enjoyed playing just a handful of games at the top level. Ironically, the day I went for a knee operation, was same date that I should have started trials with West Bromich Albion, then in the First Division (which has become the Premiership). After the operation, I never played professional football again, and will always wonder what might have been.

Saturday 18th July

Swimming lessons are cancelled due to Connor having a heavy cold.

I decide that a Press conference needs arranging at Doncaster, introducing myself and Ian Snodin to the fans and general public. I speak to Dave 'nosey' Parker, a journalist who I hope to involve in some way at Doncaster. He agrees to sort out a venue and inform the media of the event.

Unfortunately, my wife's new Marks & Spencer's credit card arrives in the post. She immediately telephones the M & S store in Handforth Dean, discovering it is open today until 8.30 pm. We'd planned a romantic evening out, only now we're going shopping, and then having a romantic evening in. We return from M&S laden with clothes. I kindly allowed her to buy me a new suit for the forthcoming Press conference. She bought herself something new for no apparent reason.

Monday 20th July

It's the first day of the summer holidays. As usual, Connor plans the day ahead, in the company of his grandmother, with military precision: 9-9.30 – cartoons; 9.30-10.00 – Sony Playstation; 10.00 food, etc.

I leave the happy scene, travelling once more to the Forte Posthouse, Brighouse – seemingly the regular meeting place to discuss Doncaster Rovers' business. I am on first-name terms with most of the staff, having been here so often-they almost have a pair of slippers and a newspaper ready for me when I appear. Today, I am meeting Paul May. We are discussing the Club's budget. Obviously, we will have to be cautious, matching the expenditure with the likely income. This is probably something new in professional sport. Most clubs appear to run at a loss, and say: 'Oh well, we must do better next year, maybe even sell somebody.'

I have known some football clubs start the season knowing they are going to lose vast amounts of money. Could this happen in any other business except sport? I doubt it. I have sat through many board meetings where most people would find the business to be unbelievable. At one meeting, we discussed a £1m. debt, but a following agenda item mentioned paying £60,000 for a player. On another occasion, I've witnessed one director walk out after another would not take seriously a discussion on catering – there were not enough cakes or sausage rolls on the boardroom buffet.

'Professional sport' is an oxymoron at many clubs. In future, many, like Bradford Park Avenue, Accrington Stanley and-more recently – Maidstone, Newport County and Aldershot, will cease to be 'professional clubs', either slipping down the leagues or into oblivion. The big clubs will simply eliminate the smaller ones, the gap between them continually widening. Also, I believe the days of a Club climbing up the leagues, as Wimbledon once did, are over.

Paul May and myself agree an initial budget for Ian Snodin to recruit players. We want to start on a very tight budget but, as we don't know whether we will get 200 or 2,000 fans per game, it is difficult to gauge. Crowd figures last season were down to a few hundred. Any money generated from gate receipts will have to be ploughed back into recruitment of players and key staff. At the moment, the club has five full-time professionals, most of which have little first team experience and Ian Snodin does not wish to retain them, several YTS lads (Doncaster is not allowed to recruit any new people this year and the best one has signed for Coventry), a chief exec., a manager, a secretary, two part-time admin. staff, and a part-time stadium manager.

Paul and I are joined by Peter Tunks, after he offered to help in the recruitment of players for Doncaster Dragons, who we hope to takeover in a few weeks time.

The meeting concluded, I depart, driving to Doncaster and a meeting with Ian Snodin. I arrive early, so tour round the town trying to spot large businesses who may want to become involved with the Club.

Once I'm with Ian, we discuss the tactics for Wednesday's Press conference and, while our announcement may not make 'News at Ten', the meeting will certainly draw a crowd. Ian tells me of the difficulty he's having recruiting players. Few in the league want to play for a Conference side, let alone one with a reputation like Doncaster's. But, with over 500 players available this summer – the first one where the Bosman ruling is in place – there are still plenty of opportunities. I agree to him holding a couple of trial games early next week and I will check on insurance for the players in case of injuries. I head home in my wife's Nissan Micra, which I'm using due to there being a fault on my own vehicle. It's a nippy little thing, but obviously not designed for someone of my stature – enough said. And, convinced that Man. United chairman Martin Edwards also has a Micra, I drive over the hills to sunny Oldham. On the way, I speak to John Bowden, a former Oldham Athletic team mate, who is now a physio and looking for a new job. We discuss a salary and I recruit him, subject to references but, as I know him,

this will be a mere formality. On parting company, I wonder how he will react to having me as a boss, though we have always got on well together. He is definitely a character, and will be popular with the players, joining in with their mickey-taking just as he did at Oldham.

Tuesday 21st July

I arrive early at Premier Crew to 'fine tune' the impending Press announcement. Having been informed that people from Sky Sports will attend, I become concerned about my clothing, hair and everything else. Knowing that television tends to make people look 12lbs heavier than they are, I decline lunch in the hope this will help me lose 3 stone overnight. Again, I speak to the head of the supporters club, invite him to the Press conference and arrange a meeting afterwards for a brief chat. I also invite Graham Patterson, a community policeman – not that I'm expecting any trouble, but it's always good to have the Law on your side. I arrange to have his favourite digestive biscuits, just to be friendly.

John Bowden, Rovers' physiotherapist
(Photo by Paul Gilligan).

July 1998

I meet Jeanna Maxwell who will work on education and community projects, having experience in gaining funds from Government and European sources. She agrees to attend tomorrow and, hopefully, meet someone from Doncaster Council.

Wednesday 22nd July

I rise early as, today, will be a big occasion for me, the new chief executive of Doncaster Rovers – from 1 August. The press conference, introducing Ian Snodin and myself to the general public, is being held at Doncaster's Grand St Leger Hotel, named after the annual St Leger horse race, dating back to 1776. I take a little longer than usual, showering and shaving, and putting on my new clothes, I believe that I've not seen the like since my wedding day. Preened and ready – I even smell nicer than usual – I tip-toe downstairs, trying not to wake the kids, and set off, full of expectations. I think back to previous Press conferences I have attended, though assume none will match the one ahead. I wonder if it will be well attended, will journalists view the take-over in a positive light and, indeed, will they see me as the right man for the job? I guess that the choice of Ian Snodin as manager will be a popular one. But, are there to be any more demonstrations by fans? There were plenty last season. After all, we have still not announced the identity of the directors or shareholders. With the fans, these are very emotive issues, and ones which I imagine will remain so until details are given. I meet David McKnight and we discuss our strategy for the day.

Ian Snodin arrives and the three of us briefly rehearse answers for the difficult, or trick, questions that may arise. David agrees to give an introduction, mentioning that on or after 1st August, when we take-over, the new directors will also hold a Press conference. They will give frank and honest answers to any questions asked and also meet the various supporters clubs.

Ian and I set off for the Grand St Leger, passing Belle Vue on the way. We both notice the poor state of the ground, Ian probably more so than me, as he began his playing career there.

'How can anybody question the logic of building a new stadium?' I ask.

'It can't come quick enough,' he replies.

On noticing the hotel's car park is full, I pull up several hundred yards away along the road. At the same time, I access the messages on my mobile 'phone. One is from Ian Green and I return his call. I chat to him for a while before passing the phone to Ian Snodin, who speaks, for the first time, to a consortium member, other than myself.

After ending the call, we get out of the car and walk to the hotel. When the Press see us, we are besieged, almost as if we are famous pop stars. We act casually, brushing aside the usual, predictable questions and enter the room allocated for the Press conference. There are around 30-40 people present, including two television crews and numerous journalists.

Ian Snodin and myself on the way to the Press conference at the Grand St Leger Hotel (Photo by Shaun Flannery).

July 1998

I stress that today's meeting is concerned with announcing the Club's new management structure, which will deal with matters both on and off the field. I ask if there are any questions, and it seems an age before anyone replies. During the silence I wonder whether this is a journalistic technique to make us feel uncomfortable or maybe catch us off guard, before asking some awkward probing questions. I consider that several enquiries are answered adequately by the three of us when, an elderly gentleman, the assistant groundsmen, introduces himself. While I'm wondering why we are not honoured with a visit from the head groundsman, I muse that the people in his job are all alike. My opinion has been formulated through many years in professional sport, working at home and abroad. I've also noticed that groundsmen are very similar to the eccentric character played by Bill Murray in the Caddy Shack film. Every professional player's dream, particularly those just starting their career, is to play on the 'first team' pitch, if only for a five-a-side game, with no crowd present. Inevitably, if an unscheduled game is organised, the groundsman will appear from nowhere and scream: 'Get off my bloody pitch.'

Players will then slink away to the changing rooms, accepting defeat once more at the hands of the groundsman. Why these people wield such power is bewildering. In my time, I have seen and been involved in many heated debates between groundsmen and players, coaches and administrators. Doncaster's assistant groundsman aims his questions at me and they are concerned with top soil, mowers and God knows what else. He also points out that repairs to the 'antique' mowers had come out of his own pocket. Clearly, he is right that these various problems need addressing, though did concede he had caught me unawares with his questions, for which, in due course, I promised some answers. Thankfully, the remainder of the Press conference passes without a hitch and, on the way out, a man called Ray Thomas introduces himself. I recognise him as a member of the 'Save the Rovers' campaign, who spoke in the Channel 5 documentary. He mentions that his boss/friend, John Ryan, head of the Transform Medical Group 'may' be interested in providing sponsorship for the Club. John Ryan's business headquarters are based in Cheshire, only a two minutes drive away from David McKnight's offices.

At lunch, Ian and I discuss the Press conference and I ask him about John Ryan. Ian says, some years ago, he was on the

John Ryan (Photo by Shaun Flannery).

Board, but did not get on with Ken Richardson. John Ryan is a 'gentleman' and has always been a fanatical Rovers supporter.

Afterwards, we buy a copy of the local evening paper – the *Doncaster Star*, whose front page headlines announce that Ian Snodin is the new manager and Alan McMahon, the chief executive. Thankfully, on the back page, I'm referred to as Ian McMahon.

At least, we have captured the front and back page headlines, showing that perhaps the Press have attached some importance to this development.

Still slightly frustrated at the typographical error, I drive homewards, wondering if the mistake is an omen. I show my wife and children the newspaper articles. The kids are impressed, even pausing from eating their Linda McCartney's country pie – for about five seconds – then continue.

Thursday 23 July

I intend spending all day on my university dissertation, a 5,000-word assignment on intellectual property rights, together with my proposal for next year's 20,000-word thesis – sports players as limited companies. I am distracted for around two-and-a-quarter hours, chatting on the telephone and, as the time reaches 11 am, I have not written a word. This, seemingly, sets the pattern for the day, as there follows numerous discussions with the Press, solicitors, directors and, of course, Ian Snodin who has coped well in his first few days of management. In time, I am sure he will prove to be a success.

Friday 24 July

I am involved in a golf tournament, and it's good to get away for the day. At 6.15 pm, a message on my mobile makes me return a call to Mark Weaver, Doncaster Rovers' general manager (until 1 August, the prospective take-over day). For some reason, known only to himself, he has arranged a pre-season friendly with Worksop Town on Wednesday. To my mind, as we have no players, the game is a pointless exercise.

Monday 27 July

Another trip to Doncaster-via Ferrybridge Services, near Pontefract. The M62 is unbelievably quiet, and I ponder the day ahead, not to mention the forthcoming season. Occasionally, 'reps' flash their headlights at me, even though I'm cruising at about 80 m.p.h. Everyone is brought to heel by the appearance of a police car in the distance, their break-lights glowing. Surely, if motorists travelled at 60 m.p.h., traffic would flow freely – or so a recent survey suggested. I plod on, turning up the volume on the 'quality' tracks occasionally played by the various radio stations, discovered while surfing the air waves.

I am a member of the Stags Golf Society and, next year, a golfing extravaganza is planned to either Dublin or Portugal. Several Society members who, like me, cruise the UK highways, also belong to the Air Miles club – no, not the mile high club – as one friend

DONCASTER Star ☆

Wednesday, July 22, 1998   28p

Ian Snodin – former captain comes home

Snodin takes over

'We are going to get back in the League'

FORMER Doncaster Rovers skipper Ian Snodin has today finally been unveiled as the club's new manager.

He will be joined by new chief executive Alan McMahon – who has wide experience in professional sport as a player and as a consultant and has worked for Hull City and Halifax Town.

Both men will take their posts from August 1 when the takeover deal by new owners Westferry Ltd is completed.

It ends months of speculation as to whether former England U21 star Snodin would be appointed.

He will now lead the club's efforts to battle its way back to the Football League after relegation last season.

Snodin, aged 34, said: "Doncaster Rovers mean a lot to me and I am excited about this.

"I have no problems at all with the new takeover and I have been assured of certain things. Hopefully we are going to work together to get Rovers back into League football.

"I have been speaking to players for the last five days before the job was finalised. League players are my priority. I want to get League players who can play a bit and good young lads as well. I used to watch Rovers last season and was appalled at the standard. It was a joke."

Sports agent David McKnight said it was the intention of the new owners to

BY DAVID KESSEN

make substantial resources available to Doncaster Rovers to get them into the League as soon as possible.

Supporters this morning welcomed the appointment of Snodin. Fan club chairman Ken Avis said he thought all supporters would be over the moon with the new manager and would rally round the club.

He said: "Hopefully Ian's arrival at the club will herald a new era because he has gone on record as saying he would never return while ever the old regime was still in charge."

It was also revealed that the club's new owners are still planning to buy Doncaster Dragons.

Save the Rovers Action Group chairman Richard Haley said he thought Snodin would be influential.

■ Snodin's hopes: Back page

Alan McMahon – new Rovers chief executive

WEATHER P20 STARS P22 BREAKTIME P24 TV P26 SHOWBUZZ P29 WHAT'S ON P30 SPORT P44-52

Front page of the Doncaster Star, Wednesday, 22 July 1998.

July 1998

assumed. For every £1 spent on petrol we receive one point. On gaining 200 points, this converts into 25 air miles. This means, if we spend £5,600, we receive a free flight to Dublin. Alternatively, spending around £9,000 will get us a freebie to Portugal. Considering my annual fuel bill will be around £4,000, a flight from Manchester to Leeds/Bradford airport may be my only option. As a businessman, I ponder on the financial advantages of being a member of this club …

As usual, I arrive early for the meeting, picking up several newspapers to read. I also buy some coffee, drinking huge amounts during each day. Some people like tea, I prefer coffee.

Rumours continue in the sports pages of Man. Utd. offering £8m, plus Andy Cole, for Dwight Yorke. Obviously, Doncaster Rovers won't be making a higher bid. We couldn't afford the interest – on his wages.

Ian Snodin turns up and we set off for Pontefract to meet his uncle, the managing director of a local Vauxhall dealership. If things go well, he will provide us with two vehicles, if they don't, we'll try somewhere else. I think that image will play a crucial part in the rise of Doncaster Rovers, or Rag Arse Rovers, as somebody put it. So, Ian and myself need two shiny new vehicles to help us get around. Frustratingly, Ian's uncle feels that he is unable to help us. He points out there is a Vauxhall dealership in Doncaster and we will have to make an approach to them.

At lunch time, back in Doncaster, we meet John Dinn at the Grand St Leger Hotel (his father Karim owns the place) along with John Bowden, Doncaster's new physio. Pleasantries are exchanged and we sit down to a rather splendid meal, the conversation straying between business and fun.

On the serious side, two players have agreed to sign for the Club. Ian is excited and, hopefully, they will be the first of many. I confirm the contract details and, when I telephone consortium member Paul May, relating them to him, the go ahead is given.

Ian's first managerial signing is Mark Hume, a 6' 3" colossus from Barnsley who, at 20, still has time to grow even taller. As we won't technically own Doncaster Rovers until 1 August, Mark actually signs for Westferry. All the Westferry signings will belong to Doncaster Rovers once the deal goes through.

The second player to sign is Shaun Goodwin, recently with Rotherham United. Ian rates him highly and has already pencilled him in as Club captain.

John Bowden is shown the training facilities we are hoping to use, including those at the Dome – a truly fantastic leisure facility – and he is very impressed. Another car dealership rep. has spoken to Ian and is very keen to be involved with sponsorship, providing a suitable advertising package can be agreed. Ian negotiates two Rover 400's for the use of himself and me.

Connor's first day at soccer camp.

'How did it go?' I ask.

'Brilliant,' he replies.

Obviously, the 'David Beckham' shirt he wore, worked wonders.

July 1998

Tuesday 28 July

A big day in McMahon Towers as Nolan Michael is three-years-old. We attempt to sing happy birthday to him, only he shouts, shut up. Children – you have to love them. His presents include a Power Rangers Turbo Mega something or other, police cars, aeroplanes, games, sweets and clothes. His favourite birthday card is a musical one which plays happy birthday. It is from my mother, who has a habit of buying this type of thing. Despite having an endless number of expensive presents, his favourite one is a £2.99 aeroplane, his face lighting up with delight when playing with it.

I work from home today, until my friend Chubby calls round. He has just separated from his partner and I agree to view a flat with him at 2 pm. At 2.10 pm the estate agent has not appeared so Chubby contacts him. Unfortunately, the agent tells Chubby he has turned up a day early, and there is no possibility of viewing the property today. Showing no sign of making any extra effort to help a customer, the agent is not going to be the next Bill Gates.

Later in the afternoon, I receive a telephone call from someone wanting a trial with Doncaster Rovers. There's nothing odd with that, only this chap has a Dutch-American accent. I learn he has been playing for Miami Fusion, a major USA league soccer team. He tells me he has won three international caps with Holland. After falling off my chair, I pick myself up again. Is this a wind up, or just someone trying their luck, or is it true Doncaster Rovers have become world famous? He mentions he has been offered a contract in Columbia, but has rejected it. He probably fears becoming another Pablo Escabor – the player who was shot dead for scoring an own goal in the World Cup.

It turns out that his grandparents, and a few relations, live in Doncaster. He wants to come to the town for a four-week trial, free-of-charge. I enquire about his level of fitness, height and the position he plays. He's 6' 1", can run 100m in under 11 seconds, and he's a forward. His name is Mason Van Basten. And, yes, he is related to the noted Dutch international, on his mother's side. I am unsure whether to be excited or not. This guy could turn out to be a clown, trying his luck with both the Club and myself. But, we have nothing to lose.

I explain I will speak to Ian Snodin, and arrange for him to play tomorrow at Worksop. Ian and I agree we will be able tell whether he is class or not after the first minute. If he is OK, we will substitute him, and lock him in a room until he signs the appropriate forms.

The first sponsorship deal is agreed. David McKnight has worked something out with John Ryan. Page 3 girl Melinda Messenger once had her assets improved by John's company and he agrees to sponsor the Club's executive lounge. Disappointingly, the Dixon-Rover deal is not going so well. However, Asics have donated some boots and training gear and may well sponsor the playing and training kit for the season. I have also talked over a potential deal with Channel 5, which made a documentary about the Club during its fall from the Football League. They will follow DRFC during the forthcoming season. It's good news, possibly encouraging sponsors to become involved with the Club. We shall see.

Wednesday 29 July

It's relatively quiet at home, and Chubby drives me over to Doncaster. This allows me to sort out some paperwork on the way. Earlier, we spent some time looking at lease cars. I will have to acquire one very soon if we cannot find a sponsorship deal. I have an allowance for a lease car but, obviously, a sponsored one makes more sense.

I arrive early at the Grand St Leger to meet Ian Snodin, finding it is packed, due to a race meeting being held tonight. I can't help but notice there are some fine fillies on show.

Ian Snodin is talking about players to David Speedie, a former Scotland and Liverpool player, now a FIFA-registered agent, based in Doncaster. In time, I receive a call from Kevin Phelan who is at Belle Vue with Mark Weaver. I join them, getting my first look inside the ground. Although a lot of work needs to be done, it is much better than I imagined. Potentially, there are four excellent bar areas upstairs and, if they are developed properly, will generate much needed revenue. The majority of renovation work needs to be undertaken in the dressing rooms, making them more 'homely'. The pitch is in great condition and, overall, I would give the ground six out of ten. It is, without question, far better than I thought. I depart quite enthusiastic about Doncaster Rovers' future, particularly from a commercial point of view.

Tonight, hopefully, should be the last time Mark Weaver & Co. are in charge at a Doncaster Rovers game-away to Worksop. Ian Snodin has arranged for several trialists to take part. As for 'Van Basten', he doesn't show. We arrive at Worksop's tidy little ground to discover they play in yellow, and the only shirts we have managed to obtain are the same colour. Mark Weaver also informs me that, yesterday, he bought 15 pairs of yellow shorts. To top that, he's brought along about 20 players of his own, including several who were 'paid up' at the end of last season. It's not the ideal start to the game which, without doubt, is the worst I have ever seen. However, there's good news – two or three of Ian's trialists are impressive. M. Weaver gets a police escort from the pitch, which is probably the most exciting part of the evening. For the record, the result is a 2-2 draw, which gave Ian and myself an indication of the team's standard over the last season – abysmal. After the game I am asked by fans if it is true that the take-over has been delayed for two weeks. I refute that, thinking it's unbelievable how people gather their information.

Thursday 30 July

At 11.30 am, I meet with Ian Snodin who says he has bad news. I expect the worse, fearing he is about to resign. He gives me details of the contracts held by the five players already on the Club's books. We both agree these may pose difficulties, though our only option is to see how the players perform on the field, before making any far-reaching decisions.

Later, I speak to David McKnight, giving me very interesting news. John Ryan (of Transform) wants to be more involved, saying if we can bring Glynn Snodin to the Club, he will pay his wages.

In the same day, we sign two more players: Colin Sutherland, a very tough Scottish centre-half, who has been playing for Scarborough; and Scott Maxfield, a Doncaster lad and a former Rovers player, recently released by Hull City.

After lunch, at the Grand St Leger, I have an appointment with a Vauxhall dealer, negotiating details with a very pleasant salesman, who says: 'I'll have to ask my boss and will get back to you.' Where have all the decision makers gone? Yes, I know that sounds impatient, but we need items like cars, balls, kit etc, now, not tomorrow.

Good news. Asics have informed Ian that they will support us, and want to have further dialogue.

Someone at Radio Sheffield 'phones at 8.30 am, wanting to discuss a Doncaster Rovers Press release which states that the Westferry take-over has been delayed. Wondering what the hell is going on, I contact Kevin Phelan and David McKnight. It transpires that Doncaster Rovers are the subject of a major Inland Revenue investigation. This means that the contract agreed with Dinard (the company holding the Club) cannot be completed under the existing terms. Westferry agreed to take on a certain amount of debt and a specified weekly wage bill. Dinard are unable to reveal the amount owed to the Inland Revenue. It could be either £40,000 or £4 million.

At midnight, a compromise is reached. On 1 August, all new debts will be met by Westferry, until the deal is 'fully' completed, which may take up to two weeks.

Fans help to spruce up Belle Vue (Photo from Sheffield Newspapers).

Friday 31 July

This morning, I point my limousine in the direction of Cheshire, for a gathering with Paul May, Kevin Phelan, David McKnight and Peter Tunks. Eventually, after discussing the way ahead for both Doncaster Rovers and Doncaster Dragons, we agree a Press release. So, with lines of communication and responsibilities established, there should be no problems as I walk into the Club on Monday morning.

Paul May will act as the overall boss of Doncaster Rovers, and answer directly to the investors. I will handle the day-to-day running of the Club, while Ian Green will act as chairman until, it is hoped, a local businessman is recruited.

David McKnight is convinced that John Ryan will be interested if Westferry show the right commitment. And, who knows, he may become the new Jack Walker. Meanwhile, Mark Weaver has called off tomorrow's friendly game with Boston United. In some ways, this signifies the old regime is over and a new one is about to start.

At night, I celebrate the take-over, having high hopes for Doncaster Rovers, not to mention myself.

24 YORKSHIRE POST
SATURDAY AUGUST 1 1998

Richardson hold on Rovers finally broken

Richard Rae

DONCASTER Rovers fans should wake this morning to the knowledge that their club is finally free from the grasp of a man under whom it has plunged through a series of disasters to the brink of extinction.

At midnight last night ownership was due to transfer from the disgraced Isle of Man-based businessman Ken Richardson to a new consortium, headed by a venture capitalist called Ian Green.

But before fans start celebrating, a substantial fly has emerged in the ointment in

the form of the Inland Revenue.

With impeccable timing, the taxman has chosen this moment to launch an investigation into the club's accounts for the past six years.

As a result a dispute has arisen between Dinard, the company Richardson used to control Doncaster, and Westferry, the name adopted by the buying consortium, over who is responsible for any potential liability.

Under the contract, Westferry agreed to take over Doncaster's debts up to a maximum of £40,000, but that was before news of the Inland

Revenue investigation emerged.

Thankfully for Doncaster fans, the dispute seems to have arisen too late to stop the deal completing. Dinard will be legally responsible for any liability over £40,000, and the new board of directors should be in place today.

The new owners are businessmen used to making a profit. The sale of the ground and the building of a new stadium, in conjunction with the council, are a central part of their plans for the club, but fans will not mind that if it means money for the team – which apparently it does.

Ian Green, who holds 96 per

cent of the new shares, specialises in refinancing and restructuring companies on behalf of banks. He will be acting chairman until the Board appoint 'a non-executive chairman more familiar with the local community and its sporting needs'.

The name of Ray Gilbert, prominent in the fans fight to save their club, has already come up in this respect.

The other new directors are Northampton-based businessman Paul May, who will serve as company secretary, and chief executive Ian McMahon, a former player who now acts as a consultant to both football and rugby league clubs.

News item from the Yorkshire Post, Saturday, 1 August 1998.

August 3 Monday

It is finally agreed that Westferry will 'run' Doncaster Rovers from today, with the proviso that any debt, incurred from this date, will be met by the company. I drive over the 'tops', through the fog and rain, wondering if I will encounter the same conditions during the year ahead. I arrive early and introduce myself and Ian Snodin to the staff, which includes Joan Oldale (Club secretary), Barbara Foster (part-time secretary), Tracey Fernie (part-time administrator), Peter White (groundsman), Ken Westfield (part-time assistant groundsman), Albert Paget (Safety Officer).

I state that we intend to forget what has happened at the Club in the past and move forward, adding that I will try to have a word with everyone, individually, over the next few days.

My first chat is with Club safety officer Albert Paget, who has a list, highlighting the urgent matters which require attention before a safety certificate can be issued. We agree to have a further meeting tomorrow.

I speak to Paul May who arranges for a builder to deal with the items on Albert's list. I am also shown another list, detailing the requirements the Conference insists on being met before we are allowed to play a game.

Hang on a minute. Are they telling us our ground is not even up to Conference standard? Yes.

I tell the groundsman to pull down all the unsightly advertising boards on the front of the main stand. Let's, at least, have the place looking like a professional football club.

For me, the rest of the day is uneventful, spending most of the time on the telephone, in meetings and working out what we need to achieve over the next two weeks. This latter splits into two areas: the recruitment of players, and acquiring a safety certificate for the ground, allowing us to play a fixture.

Tuesday 4 August

Ian Snodin holds his first training session, albeit with a few trialists.

For me, it's meetings and more meetings. I'm still trying to find a 'vehicle' sponsor and meet Barry Ellis of Exchange Car & Van Hire. He is a very lively man, agreeing to rent a car to me until I find a suitable deal. He is also interested in sponsoring the Club in some way.

In the afternoon, I see Eric Randerson, the Club's football in the community officer. Without a doubt, he worked

Groundsman Peter White (Photo from Sheffield Newspapers).

wonders under the previous regime to continue his job. We agree a strategy for the season, starting with a £1 entry for kids at the first home game against Southport on 18 August. The ticket will also give them free entry, a few days later, at the Kidderminster match.

Tonight, we're playing away at Brighouse Town, in a pre-season friendly. I arrive at their ground at 7.00 pm, parking in a field. The game starts without Ian Snodin, whose debut is delayed due to being stuck in traffic on the way back from negotiations with a player

As he wants a £25,000 signing on fee, I don't think we'll be taking him. We win the game 1-0 with impressive performances from a Tunisian lad, and another one who reminded me of Rio Ferdinand. On the way home, I remember I have not eaten a morsel all day, choosing a veggie whopper from Burger King and it's superb.

Wednesday 5 August

To me, it seems there is a permanent fog layer between Saddleworth and Holmfirth, the sunlight appearing just beyond. The twilight zone perhaps?

I am able to endure the long journey journeys to-and-from Oldham with the help of music. I have a very Catholic taste and, the music I play, usually fits my mood at the time. I don't like Donny Osmond or the Bay City Rollers, but list the following as being amongst my favourite bands/performers: Hootie and the Blow Fish, Puressence, Underworld, Joy Division, Van Morrison, John Cooper Clarke and Eric Clapton.

I once read a statistic, stating that more beer was consumed in 'country and western' bars than any other. This was due to the sadness people experienced whilst listening to the music. I concluded that C&W music could not be played in football grounds,

Eric Randerson (back row centre) and his staff (Photo by Paul Gilligan).

least of all in managers' offices, or it would cause acute alcoholism.

10.00 am – A meeting has been arranged with John Smith's Brewery to discuss possible sponsorship. Those present include Peter Tunks, David McKnight and David Parker, our media guru. I appear later on, showing them round the ground. The brewery people leave, promising to send us some figures to consider.

Ian Snodin gives me some good news – his contact at Asics says the company might be interested in sponsoring the kit. Unbelievably, Doncaster Rovers do not own a kit and I am desperate to find a kit manufacturer to sponsor us. If I fail, Dave Parker says he can borrow a kit from one of his contacts.

I see Ray Green from Doncaster Dragons – who we are buying in the next few weeks – to discuss many areas of concern, including sponsorship/marketing opportunities.

August 1998

Another pre-season game-this time with Gainsborough Trinity. Our physio John Bowden manages to acquire some old shirts and socks, but alas, no shorts. We have to purchase some before making our way to a very sunny Gainsborough.

The game ends in a creditable 1-1 draw, and I don't arrive home until 12.30 am.

Thursday 6 August

Another day and another meeting with representatives from a brewery – this time they're from Mansfields'.

A news interview with ITN about our relegation from the football league.

A full day spent with Paul May, going through plans, budgets and points to consider about the ground. The cost of carrying out safety work and adhering to Conference guidelines, enabling us to start the season, will amount to £30,000.

Season ticket sales are going well, which is a good sign, indicating that some fans believe in what we're trying to achieve.

Paul and myself seem to be striking up a very good working relationship, and I am looking forward very much to the challenge of the following months ahead.

Friday 7 August

On the way to work, I encounter fog again, though no rain. I struggle to find a decent radio station and, even when I'm lucky, the reception is poor.

There is a mountain of work on my desk and, with me having appointments all day, it'll probably still be here on Monday.

Fortunately, my first appointment is cancelled. Later, I receive a very encouraging call from David McKnight who says John Ryan wants to meet myself, along with Ian and Glynn Snodin. Ian wishes to bring his brother Glynn to the Club as his assistant, the Barnsley job having fallen through. Glynn's present club Scarborough are asking over £30,000 compensation. That price probably put Barnsley off, and it is certainly too steep for us. Nevertheless, we will discuss this and other matters.

I inform Ian of the projected meeting at Transform's Cheshire offices, before setting off for a discussion over lunch with Mike Davies, general manager of the *Doncaster Star*. I arrive ten minutes late, due my failure to understand how the town centre's pedestrian system works and difficulty in finding a suitable parking place. Usually, I am never late, and resent people who are, yet we have an excellent meeting and a deal is agreed. I receive advertising space in the *Doncaster Star*, in return for the newspaper having space, around Belle Vue, for the same purpose.

So, after garlic bread and a particularly good vegetable calzone, I return to the ground at 2.00 pm. Ian and myself are joining John Ryan at 4.00 pm, though I feel we may be late, when we encounter traffic congestion on the way.

We arrive at 4.15 pm, which is not too bad I suppose. We discuss the possibility of Glynn

Snodin and other players joining the Club, as well as more general matters. John Ryan definitely wants to play a big part in Doncaster Rover's future and is to be announced as the new chairman in the next week or so. He has invited along former Manchester City legend Mike Summerbee to inform us if any players from that club are available. John also agrees to try and persuade certain players to join Doncaster Rovers. His list includes Chris Waddle, Dailian Atkinson, and Tommy Wright. Signing any one of these would be exciting to say the least.

At 6.30 pm, there's still no sign of Glynn, obviously stuck in traffic. He's no mobile 'phone, so there's no way we can contact him. We just have to sit and wait. At 6.55 pm, he arrives, and we chat about players, coaches and the way ahead. John wants to continue the discussions over dinner and invites us to Marcello's in Hale, the home of many professional footballers. We travel there via John's Bentley, putting my Escort to shame. John is an ardent Rovers fan and reminds Ian and Glynn about some of their outstanding performances in the past for the Club. Over dinner, we agree terms with Glynn and plan how to secure his release.

Ian and Glynn Snodin (Photo by Paul Gilligan).

Monday 10 August

I see Albert Paget, the club's safety officer/stadium manager, talking over various problems, including those standing in the way of us acquiring a safety certificate.

August 1998

In the evening, I attend a supporters group gathering, having a question and answer session. I've anticipated many of the points that are raised: Is Richardson still involved? Who are the actual owners?

Eventually, the night passes off quite calmly.

Tuesday 11 August

More paperwork, and the prospect of signing additional players is discussed with Ian. With the first league game on Saturday fast approaching, we desperately need people of real quality. During the evening, we play at Eastwood Town, near Derby – the penultimate pre-season friendly. A strong Rovers team gains a good 2-2 draw, despite dominating all the game. One player attracts my attention but, alas, he's not one of ours. I ask about his availability, though with a price tag of around £20,000 on his head we will probably not pursue the matter any further. Surely, the amount they're asking is silly money, but obviously, they don't think so.

Nevertheless, we have agreed terms with our Tunisian player Noureddine 'Dino' Maamria and he played a major part during the evening's game.

Wednesday 12 August

More paper work, never leaving the office all day.

Tommy Wright has been training with us and signs up for a month. After that, who knows?

Ian asks if it possible for the team to stop overnight in Dover before the game later in the week. I feel it is a good idea, provided it is not too expensive, as we've not got any money to throw around.

Thursday 13 August

A long day ahead, with Kevin and Paul trying to finalise figures for the take-over. They need to be completed by tomorrow, or the present owners will regain control – and that would be an absolute disaster.

Paul, Kevin and myself interview Jeanna Maxwell, presently working on a community and educational project for Manchester City. I manage to convince her there are fantastic opportunities waiting at Doncaster Rovers. After all, who wouldn't want to swap clubs?

Tommy Wright receiving very close attention!
(Photo by Paul Gilligan).

Doncaster Council Leader Malcolm Glover and myself
(Photo from Sheffield Newspapers).

The three of us meet the leader of Doncaster Council, Malcolm Glover, in the town's Mansion House, informing him of our plans. He's a Rovers fan and the meeting goes well. On the way out, we bump into several Rovers supporters groups who also have an audience with the leader.

More discussions about the take-over continue throughout the afternoon and early evening. At 8.00 pm, Kevin agrees to meet Mark Weaver and talk further about any contentious issues.

A coach company sends one of their executive vehicles for us to have a look at. Very nice, and we decide it will be suitable for the Dover trip.

Friday 14 August

The season begins for us today as, a little later on, we travel to Dover, staying overnight, before tomorrow's game. I have been informed that Mark Weaver's directors have insisted he gets his own players ready to travel south, just in case the take-over doesn't go through. Now that will be interesting, not least explaining to our team that they can't play. Even if they don't, I've seen an up side to the situation. We can all nip over to Calais for some nice wines.

I am informed by Paul May that the players should board the coach and set off, just in case there are any problems. I speak to Ian Snodin, discovering it is difficult to leave before the scheduled time of 1.00 pm.

At 12.30 pm, Mark Weaver walks in and my heart beats like a kettle drum, fearing the worst. But, he is here to meet one of Dinard's directors, and he concedes there is no point in him sending a side to Dover, though he will do, if his directors insist. Half-an -hour later, Ian Snodin and myself agree that our vehicles may not be safe left over night on the large Belle Vue car park. So, we decide to park them at the Grand St Leger Hotel when, unfortunately, on the way there I'm involved in a collision with a female driver. We inspect the damage. Hers is not so bad, while mine is a little worse, with the bonnet quite badly dinted. I manage to pull into the hotel car park and the other driver and myself exchange names and addresses. A little later, I leave the car keys at the hotel and hop on to the coach, still shaken, with the indignity of the incident. I 'phone Barry Ellis, giving details. He is understanding, and promises to contact me after looking at the car.

Long coach journeys are, without doubt, the most torturous experiences footballers have to endure. I think the trip from Doncaster to Dover will be no exception. We are staying overnight in Maidstone – hopefully in a comfortable hotel. The journey is only made bearable by the customary game of cards. John Bowden, Ian Snodin and myself are joined by John Stiles (son of Nobby) and sports journalist Peter Catt (affectionately known as Peter the cat). John is helping on the coaching side until Glynn arrives, while Peter is along to cover the game. If he takes money off me, he won't be on the next trip.

Two more players have been added to the squad: Mark Bradley, from Hearts, has agreed to a month's trial, and Kevin McIntyre is on loan from Tranmere. Mark arrived just before we left, and we've arranged to pick up Kevin up from Watford Gap services.

When we get there, I ask Ian Snodin what he looks like.

I.S.: 'I'm not sure. I've only ever seen him once and he was wearing kit.'

I.M.: 'He could be anywhere.'

I.S.: 'He's a scouser, he'll find us.'

Amazingly, ten minutes later, he does. Whilst this is far from professional, we've only inherited five professional players, none of whom Ian may want to keep.

The hotel at Maidstone is absolutely brilliant, and the players love it. No more rag arse Rovers for us. I eventually check in, weighed down by my two brief cases and clothes.

Bad news – the takeover has not been completed. Everyone was arguing over figures, leaving it too late for the money to be transferred. I shower and open the mini bar. Well, you have to, don't you? To my horror, besides drinks, there are also packets of crisps and bars of chocolate. I've embarked on a health food routine though, as I've not eaten all day, I opt for a packet of crisps. Very wise, I muse.

Later, in the bar, I meet the hotel management and Ian introduces me to a friend of his, former Everton star Kevin Ratcliffe, manager of Chester City. His team is also staying at the hotel. During the remainder of the evening, I have a few pints, some dinner, then retire early. Returning to my room, I discover a fax from Joan, confirming that she has registered our players for tomorrow's game. I toss and turn all night, feeling a mixture of excitement and fear over how the team will perform.

Saturday 15 August

I don't usually have breakfast at home, but tend to over-eat when staying in a hotel, finding the vegetarian sausages and haggis quite edible. Before long, we're on the coach again, bound for Dover's ground. I'm sitting with Ian Snodin and the following conversation takes place:

I.M.: 'What video are you putting on?'
I.S.: 'One I've watched many times, featuring Michael Jordan.'
I.M.: 'You're kidding, he's one of my all-time heroes.'
I.S.: 'Mine too. Imagine though, being the best ever player in the NBA.'
I.M.: 'What do you mean? He's the best player in the universe. Haven't you seen Space Jam?'
I.S.: (laughing) 'Oh yes, I forgot. Mind, I have seen the film about 1,000 times.'
I.M.: 'I can virtually recall every line from the film.'

A little later.
I.M.: 'Well, we're nearly at the ground. How do you feel?'
I.S.: 'I'm absolutely terrified. I'm more nervous now than at any other time in my playing career.'
I.M.: 'We have come a long way in just a couple of weeks. I want us to be successful, though it will take time.'
I.S.: 'I just I wish I was playing.'
I.M.: 'I'm sure you didn't mention anything about being suspended at your job interview.'

Our lads are looking very dapper in their new tracksuits, paid for by cash to Asics. This method of payment is quite unusual today, though not, it seems, for Doncaster Rovers. Hopefully, in future, this will change, and we can pay through BACS. We arrive at Dover, parking a couple of hundred yards away from the Crabble ground. My first impression is that it is small, yet homely. Could this herald a new style in football grounds? I head for the boardroom, only to to be stopped by a Rovers' fan, who greets me as the new owner of the Club. That's strange, I think to myself, but if it gets me a better seat in the ground, who cares?

I meet the chairman of Dover F.C. and his fellow directors. Before the kick-off, the chairman says he wishes to give us a picture of Dover, to commemorate our first game in the Conference. A great gesture. Just before the game starts, Westferry directors, Paul May and Ian Green (who is acting chairman) arrive, travelling from their southern bases to watch Doncaster's first fixture. Today, Ian Snodin is 35, only due to a suspension, hanging over from last season, he is unable to play.

August 1998

As a former football player, I don't particularly enjoy watching games. I become frustrated, not being able to influence the action on the field – there are some people who say I never did when I was on it!

It is a miracle Doncaster Rovers are still in existence, never mind playing a game, and the team runs out to the cheers of over 300 fans who have made the long journey down here. Unfortunately, due to an oversight by John Bowden, the players are wearing shirts with East Riding Sacks printed on them. This company is owned by Ken Richardson – the most hated man (apart from Mark Weaver) in the Club's history. What a cock-up, though it is too late to do anything about it now. I hope nobody else notices. Fat chance, and I would like to know how we acquired them!

The first half ends with us 1-0 down. Considering two players

Shaun Goodwin leads the Rovers out for the first match of the season at Dover (Photo by Paul Gilligan).

only joined the squad yesterday, we can't really grumble. The second half begins with the directors and myself becoming increasingly concerned by the actions of around 20 so-called fans, singing and kicking down advertising hoardings. Unfortunately, late in the game, when the referee awards a penalty to Dover, these morons invade the pitch, fighting stewards and even the home side's goalkeeper. God knows what they hoped to achieve. Eventually, to our relief and embarrassment, they are escorted from the pitch. Who knows what the consequences of their actions will be. To aggravate matters, our newest recruit from Tranmere is sent off for using foul and abusive language. We lose the game 1-0. Dover's hospitality has been superb, and all we can do is apologise to the club's directors. If this is the first game, who can predict what else is in store.

On a television screen in the Dover Board Room, I look for the results of other teams in our league, noticing glamorous names like Forest Green Rovers and Kingstonian. No more Scarboroughs. Rochdales or Scunthorpes, though former league teams Barrow and Southport are in our division. I also catch part of the news, learning that a major bomb explosion has occurred in Omagh, Northern Ireland, killing at least 20 people. This event makes the one involving our fans at Dover pale into insignificance.

A tortuous journey home is broken by a beer stop for the lads, watching Ian Snodin's video featuring Michael Jordan, followed by another pause at a service station, allowing a sandwich or a Wimpy. Not quite how Manchester United would operate. But, one day …

Monday 17 August

A sombre day, with the Omagh bombing dominating the news. Kevin Phelan lives in Omagh, and his wife left the town centre at 1.45 pm on Saturday. The bomb exploded at 2 pm. Kevin explained that Omagh is a relatively small place, and most people knew those who were killed or injured.

I embark on another fog-bound journey, but this time in the opposite direction to the one I normally take. I have a meeting at Asics in Warrington with Steve Newell, to complete a 'kit' deal. Steve is brother of Mike Newell, the former Everton and Blackburn star. I wouldn't mind seeing him in a Rovers shirt … one belonging to Doncaster Rovers that is.

Without any doubt, if Asics had not sponsored Ian Snodin earlier in his career, we would not have got anywhere near a deal. Many kit companies knowing of Doncaster Rovers' past do not want to entertain us. Asics are willing to take a risk, and we tentatively work on a kit design. Hopeful, it can run into production as soon as possible.

On leaving, I head towards the M62, my 'phone ringing constantly. Once I obtain a car of my own I'll consider fitting a 'hands free' 'phone kit.

I walk into my office to be greeted by a pile of paper work, including bills and reminders. Many of the bills are several months old – even as far back as 1997. All the creditors must have heard of the take-over and thought it was an ideal opportunity to demand payment. I believe it is crucial that commercial staff are appointed as soon as possible, to encourage much needed funds into the Club.

There is a letter from the FA, informing us that we cannot sign any more players until we pay Southport the £7,050 owing to them. I speak to Paul May, telling him we have no option but to pay the demand. He responds by saying we do nothing until Westferry complete the deal with Dinard.

I see David Braithwaite from Elliott Workspace who provides us with several porta-cabins. Whilst they are an eye sore, this measure is necessary due to no other suitable offices being available in the main stand – still fire damaged from the blaze in 1995.

One meeting finished, another one begins, this time with Ray Green, the Dragons' commercial manager. It has been agreed between Peter Bentley – the Dragons' owner – and myself that, as Westferry will, hopefully, soon purchase the rugby club, Ray Green should work with us on relatively small projects including advertising boards, programme advertising etc. All this will generate much needed income. So, the sooner Ray joins us the better.

More paper work, after which, I arrive home relatively early at 9.00 pm. I have confirmed the arrangements and checked the details for tomorrow's game as well the major press conference we are staging. At this meeting Aiden Phelan (no relation to Kevin Phelan), the owner of Doncaster Rovers or Westferry's major investor, will announce that his company has taken over from Dinard. Aiden is an accountant, who has accumulated his wealth through various business ventures, including telecommunications. He is to declare John Ryan as Doncaster Rovers' new chairman. John has a non-executive role, but will act as a figure head for the Club, imbuing it with much-needed credibility. However, John will have no shares or be involved in the Club's day-to-day running. The person in overall charge of this is to be Northamptonshire businessman, Paul May. In effect, he will be handling it on behalf of Aiden Phelan. A considerable amount of money has been spent acquiring the Club, and another figure allocated as an operational budget. Therefore, it is essential that systems are established and adhered to from the outset, and not over reached. The intentions of Westferry are two-fold: to stabilise the Club, and to develop a new stadium. However, in time, it is hoped that, local businessmen can be attracted on to the Board of Directors. John Ryan of course, has already come forward and been invited to become chairman. Westferry will make these two intentions clear at the Press conference.

Additionally, Aiden Phelan is to announce Neville Southall as a new signing. Yes, the Neville Southall. Once again, Ian has used his powers of persuasion, with John Ryan agreeing to fund the deal. I think these details ought to grab everybody's attention.

Tuesday 18 August

A long day ahead I am sure.

During the morning, I finally get my hands on a safety certificate, achieving this having cost us £40,000, the local Council now being satisfied over a number of issues.

Paul May 'phones at 12.07 pm, announcing the take-over has been completed. On hearing the news, the office staff scream with excitement, not to mention relief, that a new era is dawning. The scenes, it has to be said, are quite incredible.

Kevin and Aiden Phelan arrive, greeting everyone. I give them a quick tour round the ground. A little later, we are joined by John Ryan, and a short meeting in the boardroom follows. In a half page feature, the *Yorkshire Post* has already announced that John is the new chairman. We go through what should or should not be said at the Press conference. Neville will join us near the close of the proceedings.

In the Grand St Leger Hotel, where the conference is staged, Aiden, John and myself make announcements and answer questions about the take-over. Richard Haley, of the Save the Rovers campaign, stands up and gives his wholehearted support to the new board. Peter Hunter, Chief Executive of the Football Conference, who is present at the meeting and is also invited to tonight's game, praises us for our achievements thus far. Once Neville has been introduced, the meeting closes and we return to the ground, preparing for the evening fixture, our first home game, with Southport.

Many fans are turning up and we hold a sweep in the office, guessing the gate figure.

Aiden Phelan, Ian Snodin, John Ryan and myself at the Grand St Leger Hotel
(Photo by Shaun Flannery).

During the previous year, figures fell to around 800, though the estimate for tonight is between 1500-1800. In preparing a budget for the season, we assumed around 1,500 people would attend each home game. At tonight's game, we are allowing kids in for a £1.

Outside the ground there is much activity and, at 6.45 pm, we sell out of programmes. Southport are managed by Paul Futcher, who I was apprenticed to at Oldham Athletic. Another familiar name on their team sheet is Dave 'Tommo' Thompson, having played alongside him, for a couple of seasons, at Rochdale.

While walking round the ground, I spot many kids with the 'face painter' – another one of our initiatives. Also tonight, we are giving away 500 free chocolate wagon wheels, and lots of other sweets.

I take my seat in the directors' box, noticing the ground looks quite full, and there are still long queues outside, waiting to get in. I run up to the police control area, being told that already the crowd stands at 2,600.

'Bloody marvellous,' says Albert, our stadium manager, in a blunt Barnsley accent.

The players enter the field, being warmly greeted by the fans, mainly from Doncaster. About 100 people have travelled from Southport. The new owners, board and chairman are announced and we receive a good response, though not one to match the news of Neville Southall's arrival at the Club. Meanwhile, fans are still coming through the turnstiles – amazing.

Neville Southall and Ian Snodin at the Grand St Leger Hotel (Photo by Shaun Flannery).

Crowd at the Southport game (Photo by Paul Gilligan).

The face painter has been at work! (Photo by Paul Gilligan).

Southport bring along 11 directors. Yes, 11 directors, it's unbelievable. Ten minutes into the first half, and I'm notified the gate figure is 3,663, bringing in receipts of over £16,000. Although the figure would not be earth-shattering for a lot of other clubs, it is for Doncaster Rovers, who many thought would not fulfil one game in the Conference. The match is OK, yet I suspect it may take several more outings before our players settle in and reach full fitness. Ian has done well managing to organise a squad for the early games, though I expect more new faces will appear over the coming months.

Southport are a reasonable team and they probably deserve their 1-0 victory. Sadly, our captain Shaun Goodwin is sent off and I conclude that refereeing standards in this league, compared with those in the Football League, are frighteningly poor. This does not bode well for the season ahead.

Driving home in the fog and rain, I muse that in future, after mid-week matches, it would be better to stay overnight in Doncaster .

I eventually reach home at midnight, seeing the house is in darkness. I trudge wearily upstairs and sit on the edge of Nolan's bed. He's fast asleep, though I tell him about my day. I expect, over the coming year, I will not see much of the two boys, or my wife. I have decided against moving the whole family over to Doncaster, as I feel it would be too disruptive for them. Connor is settled in his school, and so is my wife in her job.

Wednesday 19 August

I'm obviously tired after getting home late last night, and allow myself the luxury of leaving for Doncaster at 7.45 am instead of 7.30 am. Before I do, a cheque for £2,518, drops through the letterbox. It is payment, via a court order, from Halifax Blue Sox, for the work I'd carried out for them. Thank you. That will do very nicely. On arrival at Belle Vue, the staff receive numerous messages of congratulations from fans who have been 'phoning all morning. But, there's no time to rest on our laurels. We have another home game on Saturday and further work needs to be carried out on the ground.

A call from someone who is looking, on our behalf, at a few players in Ireland, and I agree to have a youth international goalkeeper on a two-week trial. He will arrive on Saturday.

Thursday 20 August

Recently, I acquired a CD, by Ladysmith Black Mambazo, after trying to locate it for some time. As might have been imagined, they are not from these parts, being an African group, and currently taking the world by storm. I discovered a liking for their kind of music whilst watching the classic film 'Zulu', staring Michael Caine. The Zulu's singing is something that I always remember. Hence making a tape from the CD and playing it now. I bet Man. United chief exec., Martin Edwards, doesn't listen to this type of music on the hi-fi system in his car.

My first encounter of the day is with a local radio station, putting together a match entertainment package for us. I agree to try it out for two games, assessing the response we get.

Jeanna appears, agreeing a job description, and a financial package. I will finalise these matters with Paul May at a meeting next week.

The rest of the day is taken by making arrangements to sign Glenn Kirkwood from Eastwood Town. John Ryan has agreed to fund this purchase, and several others. A price of £15,000 is eventually agreed with Eastwood – £7,500 now, and the remainder after 50 appearances. We believe it is money well spent and that he is a particularly good investment. His father takes a photograph of him, signing on the dotted line. At 21, Glenn probably thought his chance to become a professional had gone, but we have beaten off fierce competition from several other clubs, to land him. I recall signing my first contract – as an apprentice. I was thrilled at the prospect of what may lay ahead. Unfortunately, many players, fall by the wayside, later telling tales of what might have been, if only they had been more dedicated. Many players simply do not fulfil their potential, partly, it must be said, due to inadequate coaching. Hopefully, with the establishment of coaching academies, this will improve. Do ex-footballers make better coaches than schoolteachers, or vice-versa? I think both parties offer something unique. Footballers have intimate knowledge of the game while schoolteachers know how to handle children and impart information.

Yesterday, Glenn Kirkwood was working in a factory packing sweets. Today, he is a professional footballer. Roy of the Rovers stuff? Maybe.

Friday 21 August

During the morning, Ian Snodin, Joan Oldale (the Club secretary) and myself have a meeting, and I ask Joan if all our players are now registered.

'Yes,' she says, quickly followed by a 'No.'

'Oh, and who's not registered?' I probe, expecting it to be a YTS lad.

'I haven't registered Ian Snodin,' came the reply.

'Damn,' I shout, which is unusual for me as, normally, I'm difficult to rile. 'He played on Tuesday against Southport.'

Joan leaps up, scurrying away to get Ian registered.

I have the unenviable task of telling Peter Hunter, chief executive of the Conference, about our blunder. He agrees to mention it to his committee though, in view of the upheaval the Club has gone through, and the fact that we did not win Southport, he predicts there will not be any repercussions.

I take a 'phone call from one of the Doncaster Dragons directors, saying that despite the agreement between myself and Peter Bentley, Ray Green cannot work for us. This director, who I believe only has £50 worth of shares in the Dragons, claims that P. Bentley had no authority to make the deal. As Westferry will own Doncaster Dragons, sooner rather than later, I agree to cover Ray's wages.

After lunch, Ian Snodin appears in my office and I enquire about young Kirkwood's first day.

'A nightmare,' barks Ian. 'He was bloody rubbish. The lads are asking if the ink has dried yet on his contract.'

I remember my first few days at Oldham Athletic, when seasoned professionals made newcomers look very foolish. Over the years, I lost track of how many apprentices/YTS lads were asked to undertake ridiculous tasks or sent out on

Glenn Kirkwood in action
(Photo by Paul Gilligan).

bogus errands. One example of this foolish behaviour might involve telling a lad the manager wants to see him, only to find out, this is untrue. It's childish, I know.

We agree to a two-week trial for the Irish goalkeeper, who has represented his country on many occasions. John Ryan has agreed to put £20,000 into the club, only due to a fault of the system, it cannot be transferred until Monday.

Today, Dwight Yorke becomes a Manchester United player, the club having paid £12m. for him. I muse on the fact that John Ryan's £20k would probably not cover a week's wages for him. Without doubt, the top Premier League teams are creating a massive financial gap between themselves and teams in the lower leagues.

Preparations are in place for tomorrow's game, so I make my way home, hoping we can achieve our first win of the season.

Saturday 22 August

Today, I am taking my friend, Chubby, over to Doncaster, giving him the opportunity to see some real football, as he's a Manchester City supporter. Also, we decide to have a few drinks after the game, and stay the night in Doncaster.

Arriving at the ground, we witness a hive of activity, suggesting a reasonable attendance figure. We are playing Kidderminster Harriers, one of the Conference's top teams. Rovers are still not at full strength, though I'm sure Ian, who is playing today, will do all he can to raise morale. There was an unbelievable crowd at the Southport game, and I doubt whether this will be repeated today. A lot of work has been done to increase our profile locally and nationally, so we shall have to see. The half-time draw tickets are selling well and there seems to be as many people milling outside the ground, as there was the other night. John Ryan has convinced me that the team will win, and who am I to doubt such enthusiasm? I sit anxiously, watching fans enter in one by one, through the turnstiles. Children will be admitted free today, so it will be interesting to discover how many come along for the 'Donny' experience. Kick-off looms and I cannot wait any longer to learn the crowd numbers, running up to the control box.

Mascots and ball boys
(Photo by Malcolm Billingham).

Fans waiting at the turnstiles (Photo by Malcolm Billingham).

'Relax Ian, it's over 3,000,' says Albert.

Bloody hell, that's great I say to myself, skipping back to my seat, and thinking a win would cap a brilliant day. In the first half, Kidderminster are by far the better team, playing with three up front most of the time. Just before half-time, they have a man sent off for a diabolical tackle. After the interval, we press home our superior advantage and, late in the game, we are awarded a penalty. I cannot look, but Shaun Goodwin calmly takes the ball and coolly slots it home. The tension continues to mount as Neville Southall pulls off a couple of remarkable saves. When the final whistle blows, Rovers' achieve their first home win home since God knows when, and it's in front of 3,222 people. I gaze out on to the pitch, feeling as elated as both the players and the fans. I have never seen Ian Snodin looking so happy, actually skipping round the field through sheer delight. Amazingly, in such a short space of time, the mood of the fans has changed from hatred to adulation.

Colin Sutherland, who I have christened 'Begbie', after the 'Trainspotting' character, is nominated man of the match. For me, all the players did well, and any one of them might have won the award. Ian Green, John Ryan and myself take a few bottles of champagne into the players, all exhausted, but happy. The Board Room seems to have attracted a few hangers on, but this happens in football. Richard Hayley (of the Save the Rovers fame) is almost in tears. He genuinely never believed he would ever see Rovers play again, let alone win a game.

August 1998

In football, people have to enjoy the good times when they can, because there are plenty of bad times. Chubby and myself finally succumb to a drink in the boardroom.

Later, we walk over to the Grand St Leger, meeting another potential Rovers player, David Penney, captain of Cardiff City. He originates from Castleford and is desperate to return north, the Welsh fans giving him a hard time. The reason is that he signed from Swansea, Cardiff's arch rivals. Without a doubt, football is a funny old game, making men turn against each other through supporting rival football teams – even when they are based in the same city. I have never been a supporter of one particular team, so I am probably not qualified to talk any further on the subject. Chubby, a Man. City fan himself, agrees with me on that point.

At the St Leger, people are almost hanging from the rafters, as there's a wedding reception in full swing. We move to the Earl of Doncaster Hotel, a few hundred yards away. I have a lift with John Ryan, in his vehicle, and we find a room to thrash out a deal with Dave Penney. He will definitely be a valuable acquisition, Ian Snodin rating him very highly. Again, John Ryan has agreed to pay the transfer/signing on fee, otherwise Ian's budget would be soon over spent.

Monday 24 August

Nolan has been impressing us over the weekend, running around spouting the immortal Michael Caine line from the Italian Job: 'You're only supposed to blow the bloody doors off.'

Rovers fans pictured before an away game (Photo by Shaun Flannery).

I gather this is featured in a television commercial. Although everyone agrees that Nolan can mimic a cockney accent marvellously, if he continues to be 'Michael Caine' at nursery, I'm not sure how well it will go down.

Following Saturday's victory, there is a new air of optimism at the ground. We have probably taken more in gate receipts, over the last two games, than most of the fixtures last season. Long may it continue. Receipts from season tickets are now over £15k. It's not earth-shattering, but we only expected to sell between £2k-£3k. I agree a deal with Magic AM to part sponsor air time and pre-match entertainment. Hopefully, this will increase our already glowing profile within the media.

I ask Ian Snodin to check if there are any injuries, barring players from tomorrow's trip to Barrow. There's only one player injured, and it's Ian, himself. Hopefully, the injury will respond to treatment in time for him to play.

I receive many 'phone calls, saying how well the Club is now being run, after only a few weeks under new management. A few are from parents whose kids attended Saturday's match. In total over 770 under-16s were there, and it created a great atmosphere, which was especially appreciated by Neville Southall, Tommy Wright and Ian Snodin. Again, on Saturday, we sold out of programmes. The way they are selling, they could easily become collectors' items.

I speak to Gerry in Ireland, continuing our dialogue about potential players coming to Doncaster for trials.

After the morning's training session, I ask Ian Snodin how Glenn 'Gummy Bear' Kirkwood performed.

'Brilliantly' says Ian, 'he was awesome in shooting practice.'

Thank goodness for that.

Tuesday 25 August

At 6.50 am, the day already seems to be dragging, as I'm stuck behind a tractor on a narrow road. It's also foggy and wet. I eventually arrive in the office around 8.15 am where I prepare paper work for a trip with Paul May to see John Ryan at his Cheshire offices. A quick bite to eat at lunch time, and we are on our way, travelling the hour-and-a-half long torturous journey – stuck behind lorry after lorry – over Snake Pass. We turn up 20 minutes late, though agree our strategy and establish guidelines for John's input into the Club. After all, he is not a shareholder, and fully accepts the situation.

After a quick coffee, we move to John's home, parking our cars and wait while he gets changed. Meanwhile, I survey his lovely home which featured so prominently in the TV programme 'Neighbours at War'. We leave in John's Bentley turbo, confident of a comfortable and fast journey. Who would have thought, after all these years, I would be returning (and in a Bentley) to Barrow, where I played on many occasions, the last time being around 1985. Barrow itself, has not changed much, though the football ground has improved in leaps and bounds, two new stands having been built in recent years. As a

August 1998

player, I always dreaded the long journey to Barrow, though we often stopped for refreshments at one of the motorway service stations. On one occasion, we pulled in for a pre-match meal, all the players being given £3.00p to spend. Darron McDonough, bought steak pie, chips and peas and, on seeing him troughing, the coach Billy Urmson's face was a picture.

In recent years, a dual-carriageway has been constructed on the outskirts of Barrow, making the journey into the town slightly more bearable. We arrive at the ground only to be told that the main car park is full, having to use another one some distance away. Meanwhile, John tops up the car engine with oil because of a leak. It's a slightly curious sight watching a Bentley owner doing this – though if it has to be done …

The game is reasonably entertaining, ending in a 2-2 draw. We played without Ian Snodin who, as I suspected, was unfit. Paul May is now becoming a true football fan. Another addition to our party is Mike Collet, a former Doncaster Rovers director. He currently lives in Jersey and, before the game, flew to a local airfield, taking a taxi from there to the ground. This perhaps shows that Doncaster Rovers is not just an average club with an average set of supporters. After the buffet, we're on the road again, arriving back in Cheshire some two hours later. I grab my jacket from the boot only to find that oil from the can John used earlier has leaked over it. John agrees to have the jacket cleaned and I eventually crawl into bed, very late.

Wednesday 26 August

I allow myself the luxury of seeing the kids before leaving around 8.00 am. Such decadence. The journey to Doncaster is becoming boring, but I have discovered a radio station, which does not crackle or fade. So, at least I can listen to music and chat while travelling to and from work. In my opinion, Chris Evans and Virgin Radio, despite receiving a lot of bad Press, are actually very good. Normally, I am a supporter of local radio, but have made an exception, listening to Virgin Radio. However, when I'm near Doncaster, I switch to Magic AM, listening to the adverts we are running.

At 11.30 am, I see Alan Washington, who is manufacturing the kit for Asics. We agree on some designs and he also drops off another kit for us to use in the meantime. John Ryan has agreed to cover costs, providing his corporate logo can be used on it. This will be the third kit we've used.

Pat Lally, from the PFA, cancels a meeting regarding YTS players. We desperately need some, and I was hoping something could be agreed today. This will now have to wait until next week.

I have put pressure on John Ryan to step up negotiations for the release of Glynn Snodin from Scarbrough. He tells me the club have agreed to release him after their Bank Holiday Monday game.

I finally agree a contract with Jeanna Maxwell, taking care of youth and community projects.

A family atmosphere at Belle Vue (Photo by Malcolm Billingham).

I finish work early, arriving home at 8.00, as I'm taking my wife to our favourite restaurant 'Nutters', situated on the outskirts of Rochdale. It is a real family affair, being owned and run by celebrity chef Andrew Nutter and his parents. There is a real relaxing atmosphere, enabling me to enjoy my wife's company and escape momentarily from the problems of Doncaster Rovers. I always fancied being a cook myself, and my wife has often complemented me on the dishes I serve.

'But, you make such a bloody mess,' she invariably adds.

Doesn't everybody else?

Thursday 27 August

I join John Ryan and his friend Ray Thomas, both long-time Rovers fans, to discuss the appointment of Alick Jeffrey as club president. Barring Kevin Keegan, many people believe Alick, now 59, was Doncaster's greatest ever player. It has to pointed out that, whilst Keegan was at the Club, he never played any first team games.

Afterwards, we have lunch with Ian Snodin, talking about a variety of matters, including the possible signing of John Sheridan, the former Republic of Ireland international. Surprisingly, at the moment, he is unattached and we agree on John Ryan trying to persuade him to join us.

After lunch, property-letting agent, Stuart Highfield, arrives, announcing that he would like to become involved with the Club. He agrees to donate a sizeable sum for the development of a youth squad or, help assist with the Club's community projects. This is fantastic news.

August 1998

Late in the afternoon, Glynn Snodin pops in with a list of requirements for his office.

'You can have what you want in it,' I tell him, 'but there is no money. You will have to acquire items yourself.'

'All I want is £35 for a fridge.'

'No,' I say, 'anything else?'

'No bloody point,' he snaps.

There's some good-natured banter between us, though we both know there is definitely no money for such luxuries.

Friday 28 August

An early morning liaison with Steve King from Magic FM, where I agree to the radio station organising pre-match advertising and matchday entertainment for two of our games. I will have to pay for this, but hope it will attract a new audience to the Club. I'm convinced that Doncaster's large population is ready for football success. We are still several weeks away from having a full squad of players, although making steady progress.

It surprises me that many clubs outside the Premiership do not have a marketing budget. Most would not even consider appointing a marketing manager. It's amazing really. As a result of Rovers having both, I feel sure – even at this stage – we will be able to attract more fans through our gates than any other team in the Conference, perhaps even in the third division.

The call I have been waiting for eventually arrives – John Sheridan has agreed to play three games for us and will consider his options thereafter. This is fantastic.

I contact Dave Parker to send out a Press release, announcing the news.

With a bit of luck, if we win tomorrow at Kingstonian, this might encourage a good crowd at Bank Holiday Monday's home game against Kettering.

It's a good day, so far, and gets better when Stuart Highfield pops in with the first of three donations to the Club. Five minutes later, Barry Ellis 'phones, offering us three cars for the season. The deal is worth £5,000, and it's fantastic.

A relatively early finish at 7.00 pm, and I miss most of the traffic jams.

Saturday 29 August

I experience the luxury of a little extra time in bed, before heading to John Ryan's house in Great Budworth. I arrive half-an-hour early, and we are soon on our way to Kingstonian. This time, I place my jacket on the back seat, instead of in the boot, not taking any chances with leaking oil cans. The ride, as might be expected in a Bentley, is very smooth though, somehow, we mange to miss the M25 exit from the M40, because of road works, ending up in the middle of London. We travel round the West End sightseeing, even having time for the car windows to be cleaned. Neither of us have any change, so John gives the 'window cleaner' £5.

Eventually, we find the A3, making our way to Kingstonian's small, but impressive, ground. Already, there are many Rovers fans present and, I meet two who want to buy a

Republic of Ireland star, John Sheridan, in action for Rovers (Photo by Shaun Flannery).

player. As anyone might imagine, it's not every day that I deal with this type of request. I am cautious about getting too excited, until I hear what they have to say. It transpires they are brokers in the city, having a substantial disposable income, which they are willing to offer the Club in return for a place on the Board. We agree to discuss the matter further over the next few weeks.

I watch our players 'warming up' in the 'temporary kit' sponsored by Transform. It looks OK and, with the two new signings, Sheridan and Penney, I expect us to do well today. The beautiful weather is matched by Kingstonian's hospitality. Commercially, they obviously do well and there is a great atmosphere around the ground.

Neville Southall (Photo by Shaun Flannery).

The game begins and we look comfortable with the ball, though Dave Penney appears to have some difficulty blending with the rest of the team. After 20 minutes, there's a calamity. Captain Shaun Goodwin comes off injured. Nevertheless, we dominate the first half, which ends 0-0, playing the best football I have seen us produce so far. Ten minutes into the second half and a brilliant volley is saved by their keeper. Seconds later, Penney goes down, looking seriously injured. Eventually, he struggles to his feet only, two minutes later, has to come off. We lose the game 1-0 with a goal scored in the last minute. Some might argue this was the fault of Neville Southall, while he might disagree. Looking back on the game in a positive light, we hammered the opposition for almost the full 90 minutes, but lost. We are in need of striker and the sooner we get one the better it will be. In the dressing room, Ian Snodin is very disappointed and amazed that we lost. This is football.

John and I quickly attack the buffet before leaving. We stop only once, John filling up with petrol while I carry out some 'research'. Page 3 girl Amanda Robbins is modelling our new strip at next week's game with Forest Green. She is featured over several pages in this month's Loaded magazine and I sneak a peek at some of the pictures. While doing this, I feel like a pervert and that everybody is looking at me.

John and I spend the remainder of the journey discussing the positive work done at the

Club so far, the need for a striker, and how we might solve the problem..

Bank Holiday Monday 31 August

I feel delicate after spending Sunday wining and dining with my wife Elise and our two friends Alan and Steph. Initially, we planned a quiet relaxing time around Manchester, having lunch and a few drinks. But, it was Mardi Gras weekend and we all had too much wine followed by a curry later on.

As I have not seen much of Elise, Connor and Nolan over the last few months, they are travelling to Doncaster with me today. It will also give them an opportunity to watch the match, see where I work and what I get up to. Before doing that, they drop me off at the ground and head in the direction of a McDonalds.

*Ian Snodin studies the game
(Photo by Paul Gilligan).*

There is a lot happening today with Magic FM organising several events. Also, a BBC camera crew will film the game and interview Ian Snodin, Neville Southall and John Ryan.

Throughout the morning, kids are queueing up to buy the £1 tickets, on offer to them for today's match. At 2.40 pm, I am informed we have sold all the 800 tickets. Meanwhile, the pre-match entertainment is being well received by over 4,000 fans already in the ground – and the turnstiles are still clicking.

John Sheridan has invited Chris Waddle and his family to the game and we usher them into the Board Room. As yet, Chris has not signed for a club and our hopes are high for him to come to Doncaster. After all, if you don't ask, you never get, as the saying goes. Ten minutes after the kick-off, the official gate figure is 4,569. It's amazing when looking back to last season and realising the attendances were as low as 800. I definitely think we're heading in the right direction. The bad news is that Ian Snodin is unfit to play and we have four other players out for a game against a team riding high in the league. We play quite well and, while we should have won the game, it ends in a 1-1 draw. Glenn Kirkwood scored his first goal for the Club, while Mark Hume was sent off. I try not to criticise referees, but in my opinion, the one today cost us the game. I know refereeing is a very emotive subject, but each week mistakes made by part-time officials have massive consequences. Also, I hear that today's match official was refereeing a Conference game for the first time. At least the 800 or more kids had a good day, and I drive home still excited about the overall crowd and the £20k gate receipts.

Elise and the boys thoroughly enjoyed the day too.

Tuesday 1 September

Connor returns to school today, resplendent in new shoes, trousers (with perfect creases), shirt and sweater. I'll give him twenty minutes before he looks dishevelled, just like he did everyday last term. It's amazing how boys have an inbuilt ability to resemble Dennis the Menace at any given time of the day. Nolan is attending a private nursery, and I wish both boys good luck, before leaving.

Officially, it's Glynn Snodin's first day as Ian's assistant, and photographs are taken in spite of the them forgetting about the event. I feel sure the two brothers will get the Club back on its feet. Whilst it may take some time, I'm convinced it will happen. With no training today, they spend much of their time sorting out their offices, and preparing for tomorrow, when the players return.

I read through a very interesting fax message, indicating that McDonalds would like to sponsor the Club in some way. At last, we are now attracting blue chip companies.

I desperately need some commercial staff, as I am becoming bogged down undertaking this type of work myself, and all the other duties I have to carry out.

Wednesday 2 September

Early morning, I receive a call from University lecturer Mark James. He allows me to defer an assignment until December, due to my present work load. Unfortunately, if this continues to accumulate in the way it has done over the last few weeks, I may have to defer the assignment for a year.

It's Glynn's first training day, and he prepares the players for Saturday's home game with Forest Green Rovers.

I arrange to go to the Man. Utd. v Barcelona game on 16 September with John Ryan, Ian and Glynn Snodin, and maybe John Sheridan, who we hope to sign around that time.

A meeting with Alick Jeffrey Jnr, who may help with the commercial side of the Club. He is a very good friend of Ian Snodin's, and I have met him on a handful of occasions, in the past. He is, most certainly, a character and has many contacts. Hopefully, he can attract more sponsorship for us.

John Ryan agrees to pay for the bars to be refurbished.

Thursday 3 September

I leave home at 7.20 am, but don't arrive in Doncaster until a little after 9.00 am. Paul May is coming today, along with his accountant, Ian, to examine our office systems. Ian will spend most of the day with Joan Oldale, leaving Paul and myself to concentrate on various issues. We talk about paying Dave Cowling and Paul Ward the money owing to them. This is an outstanding issue, dragging on from the previous regime. We discuss the offer through ACAS and that it should be accepted.

Jeanna turns up and we finally complete her 'deal'.

The day is tinged with sadness, being the funeral of Doncaster Rovers Ladies team member Lucy Hobson who was tragically killed in a car crash last week. She was only 22.

Ian Snodin informs four of the five players, inherited from Dinard, that he is making them available on a free transfer. It's not a nice thing for a manager to do, at any level. But, managers stand or fall by their decisions. Meanwhile, contracts are offered to Tommy Wright and Jason Minett (a former Exeter City player).

Friday 4 September

Another day full of meetings. And, as time goes on, more and more of these are seemingly concerned with solving problems incurred during the Dinard days. One meeting today is regarding an unpaid bill for a photocopier.

Later, it's over to Doncaster Racecourse, situated adjacent to Belle Vue, meeting chief executive John Sanderson. Preparations are in full swing for the town's annual Race Week. I know nothing about horse racing, only thought it was worthwhile making the acquaintance of someone else concerned with sport in the town.

Good news. The first kit samples from Asics arrive. They look good – especially when considering only ten minutes was spent on our designs. During my time in sport, I have designed many shirts. They are no longer just an item of kit, worn on match days, but also a strong source of accruing advertising income. For us, it will not create anywhere near the amounts

Dave Penney (Photo by Shaun Flannery).

obtained by Manchester United, but it will be useful, nevertheless.

Details concerning our 'free transfer' players have been circulated today. The harsh financial reality for a club like ours is that we need them off the books as soon as possible.

Plans and final arrangements are made for tomorrow's game, before I wend my way home through the rush hour traffic, catching one of our adverts on a local radio station.

Model, Amanda Robbins, poses in Rovers kit (Photo by Paul Gilligan).

Saturday 5 September

An early start for the home game against relatively unknown Forest Green Rovers. They are from Gloucestershire and were promoted to the Conference last season.

Connor is with me and will be joined by Paul May's two sons. Hopefully, they will get on together and have an enjoyable time.

Today, we are honouring one of Doncaster Rovers' former players, Alick Jeffrey whose career was launched during the 1954-55 season when he was only 15. A year later he won caps at schoolboy, youth and amateur international level. He was expected to win a full England cap, being described as the Michael Owen of his era, but broke his leg whilst playing in a 'B' international. Complications followed and he was advised to retire, eventually emigrating for a time to Australia. He rejoined Rovers during the 1964-65 season, subsequently scoring 36 league goals. He continued to be a driving force with the Club for a number of years, making 262 league appearances and scoring 129 goals. During the previous regime's time, he stopped watching Rovers, but has since come back.

A meeting at 1.00 pm with someone who would like to become our Commercial Manager – a position we need to fill as soon as possible. I am very impressed with his CV, positive attitude, and enthusiasm. We agree to talk again sometime in the future.

Page 3 girl Amanda Robbins is modelling our new 'home' strip. Potential Rovers Vice-chairman and pilot Mike Collett is flying into Bristol to collect her and boyfriend. On arrival at the ground, Amanda immediately attracts a lot of male attention, females arguing 'she's not that nice.'

A group picture which includes some old Rovers stars, including Syd Bycroft, Charlie Williams, Alick Jeffrey and Laurie Sheffield (Photo by Paul Gilligan).

Ex-Man City legend, Mike Summerbee, makes a presentation to Rovers president Alick Jeffrey (Photo by Paul Gilligan).

Every seat is taken in the Directors' Box, and also in the executive area. Some of the seats there are occupied by a number of Alick's Jeffrey's colleagues who played alongside him during the 1950s and 1960s.

The game kicks off in front of another great crowd-3,402. At half time I feel it will be a bad day for us, having created at least ten good scoring opportunities, yet the score is still 0-0.

While there are many people present, the only voice I can hear above the rest is that of my son Connor. It's obvious he takes after his mother … Suffice to say, he is getting on well with Paul May's sons.

Disaster. We lose the game 1-0. Ian and Glynn are devastated. We desperately need a goal scorer and a bit of luck.

A number of players, staff, Alick Jeffrey and guests move on to the Earl of Doncaster Hotel where a buffet and 'free bar', organised by John Ryan, awaits them.

Later, I head for home, thoroughly exhausted, while Connor is still full of energy and chattering. No sooner have we travelled 200 yards than he utters those immortal words: 'Dad, can I have a McDonalds?'

I give in – anything for a quiet drive over the hills.

Monday 7 September

There is no mid-week game this week.

The Snodin brothers are still suffering from shock after Saturday's defeat. They are not quite sure how we lost, and neither am I. We discuss the need for a goal scorer. Unfortunately, they are as rare as hen's teeth. And, when good goal scorers emerge they are usually snapped up by clubs in higher divisions. The three of us agree there is no need to panic, just yet. In the meantime, Glynn and Ian will continue their efforts to find someone suitable, spending every day scouting.

Tuesday 8 September

Ian and Glynn enquire about a striker at non-league Emley. They want £30,000. Obviously, he will not be joining us. The two brothers also speak to ex-Liverpool and Spurs star, Paul Stewart. Later, his agent says Paul will sign for Doncaster Rovers providing we meet his £1,000 a week wages. Thanks, but no thanks. Given our situation, we are unable to pay that sort of money.

At 11.30 am, Stuart Highfield and myself discuss youth football in the area. It's a useful meeting, ending with Stuart suggesting we have a look at the facilities at High Melton College, situated in a rural setting – about eight miles west of the town centre. I believe it is an ideal site for a football academy, where 9-16 year old boys would, live, train and be educated. Many Premier League teams have established this kind of facility.

On the way back, I pick up my tickets for Thursday's race meeting. These have been kindly donated by Bryan Chambers, a local Mercedes Benz dealer.

I spend the rest of the day locked in discussions about academies and centres of excellence. The paper work held at Doncaster concerning the previous centre of excellence and the YTS scheme is pitiful and trying to make sense of it will be very time consuming.

I eventually finish the day around 9.00 pm, steering my rented vehicle over the Pennines.

Wednesday 9 September

The main sports story today is that Rupert Murdoch has made a £625m offer for Manchester United. Yes, £625 million, which is probably regarded as a bargain. It appears that the Manchester United PLC directors are seriously considering the offer. Will this be the first of a number of clubs sold to the media? I'm sure it's a story that will run for a long time.

Dave Parker arrives and we have a preliminary conversation before joining Steve Kerry from Thwaites Brewery. I have known Steve since my Oldham Rugby League days, where he helped set up a sponsorship deal between the club and brewery. Hopefully, something similar can be arranged here. We show him the bar areas, which are still being refurbished, and the meeting ends with Steve saying he will contact me in due course.

September 1998

In the afternoon, a call is received from Top Gear's Jeremy Clarkson, whose mother lives in the local village of Tickhill. He explains that he would like to do some filming, during a match day, for inclusion in one of his shows.

Later in the day, Ian Snodin informs me that Chris Waddle may be interested in playing for us.

Meanwhile, the players go to the races, and it will be interesting to see who are the winners and losers. Isn't it amazing that, whenever a keen race goer is asked how they have fared, they always reply: 'I have broken even' or 'I'm a little bit up.' I am definitely not a big gambler.

John Ryan and myself agree the offer to be put to Chris Waddle. Ian Snodin wants him to join us on a long-term basis, not just for a game or two.

Thursday 10 September

I am sick and tired of fog, meeting it virtually every morning. On leaving home, I'm wearing sun glasses, quickly changing them for ordinary spectacles when crossing the Pennines.

One of the players turns up for training worse-for-wear from the previous day at the races. As might have been predicted, this does not go down well with the management. The Snodins ask me what course of action they should take with the player – who shall remain anonymous.

I explain the options. We talk about these for a while, until I insist that the player is sent home. I do not need this sort of problem early in the day, but it is such fun being in charge of a football club. Eventually, a taxi arrives and he is bundled away.

Later, I attend the races with my friends Chubby, Rob, and Alick Jeffrey Jnr. During the course of the afternoon and evening: We discover that Alick appears to know every man and his dog, and we build up a list of useful contacts and possible sponsors. I win three out of six bets, we have a curry at a local Indian restaurant, and I find that the B & B, where I'm staying overnight, is in the middle of the town's notorious red light area.

It might be suggested, it has been an eventful day.

Friday 11 September

At 7.00 am, I decide to give my friends an early morning call. I don't like anybody else being asleep if I'm awake. Rob hasn't bothered to take off his suit or even his shoes before going to bed, indicating he must have had a good night. I eat a light breakfast of toast and coffee, and by 8.00 am, I'm sitting behind my desk ready for the day ahead. Glancing through the papers, I notice Bill Clinton is in trouble over the Monica Lewinsky affair, and several Doncaster councillors are being accused of allegedly fiddling their expenses in what has become known as the long-running 'Donnygate' affair.

Good news – we sign former Liverpool and Scotland player Steve Nicol, on a match to match basis. Who would have thought, several months ago, the Club would be attracting players of his calibre? He will be a welcome addition to Ian's fast-growing squad.

Much of the afternoon drifts by sorting out problems with YTS, and the day's last job is choosing the colour of the carpet for the bars upstairs. Well, somebody has to do it.

Saturday 12 September

I get up a little later than usual, before travelling over to John Ryan's house. We set off on the long journey to Hayes, Middlesex, only made bearable by the comfort of his Bentley. Our discussions centre around tactics, team selection, the players we have and those who we want – the usual rubbish club officials talk about. Two hours later, we are making the return journey, devastated after a 2-0 defeat. We definitely need a couple of forwards. No disrespect to those we've got, only I can't see any of them scoring 15-20 goals during the season.

Steve Nicol showing his skills (Photo by Paul Gilligan).

The way back is only made pleasurable by regularly dipping into a packet of pear drops, arriving home at 9.00 pm, and rounding off the evening by having a glass of wine with my wife.

Monday 14 September

Glynn and Ian are still smarting after Saturday's defeat. Everybody keeps telling us we are playing well and that they expect to see us finish in a good position at the end of the season. I only hope they are right. I finally get hold of Chris Waddle and offer him, what I believe, is a good deal. Financially, he tells me that, it does not match the one Torquay have offered. However, Doncaster is only 'down the road' from where he lives, and this is an advantage. He will consider our offer and make a decision in due course.

Tuesday 15 September

A disappointing sponsorship offer is received from Thwaites Brewery, which we will not accept.

I leave at 4.00 pm, driving towards Southport for tonight's game. I travel via Oldham, picking up my friend, Chubby, who has become quite a Rovers fan. As usual, the M62 is extremely busy

September 1998

and we find Southport's ground at 7.45-kick-off time. I search for a suitable parking place, only to discover there are none. I also notice five or six policemen, patrolling on horseback. After the 'Dover' rumpus, I suspect this is a measure to quell any similar incidents occurring. I eventually park about half-a-mile away from the ground and, on returning, find the ticket office is closed. We gain entry to the ground 10 or 15 minutes into the game, sitting near John Ryan and Ian Green.

'We're winning 1-0,' John tells me.

'What is the score really?' I ask.

'We're winning 1-0,' he repeats.

'Yes we are,' adjoins Dave Parker.

A little later, the impossible happens, we score another goal. At 2-0, I wonder if the past is finally behind us. Unfortunately, goalkeeper Neville Southall has been injured, and it appears to be worsening. We haven't a substitute goalkeeper and, when the whistle blows at half-time, he slowly hobbles from the pitch. On the way to refreshments in the Board Room, we ponder on who can play in goal.

Tommy Wright?

'Too small.'

'Dino?'

'No way. He's Tunisian.'

At that point, the cheese sandwiches come into view and everyone is distracted. Once we're back in our seats, I notice that Neville has emerged for the second half, his condition not improved. I also note that Southport are taking advantage of the situation by playing their big centre half up front. With hindsight, Neville should have been substituted but, with limited resources, what could be done? We lose the game 3-2, with Ian Snodin being sent off, to add insult to injury. Later, in the Board Room, I offer my congratulations to the Southport directors. I feel depressed. I even consider eating a steak-and-kidney pie, which appears to be winking invitingly at me, only I resist the temptation.

Wednesday 16 September

Unfortunately, a meeting with Asda has to be cancelled due to one of their representatives being ill. This is a pity, as I was keen to talk to them about sponsoring our Youth and Community Programme. My next appointment is with reps from McDonalds. I want the company to help us bring more people through the turnstiles, via promotions, give-aways and other methods. A good meeting ends with an offer on its way.

During the afternoon I make my way to John Ryan's offices, with both Snodin brothers – following behind – or so I thought. On arrival there, I'm amazed to learn that Ian is absent because of a foot injury.

'How the hell did he do that?' I ask, assuming the injury was sustained during last night's game.

'After he was sent off,' begins Glynn, 'he went into the changing room and booted the door.'

I'm not sure whether to laugh or to be extremely disappointed. I suppose being a little hot-headed is a characteristic which has made him a great player.

In the meeting, we discuss areas of concern and agree to target several players. Glynn mentions that Ian and himself are out scouting every day. But, players are either showing reluctance to come to Doncaster or asking silly wages.

One of the main purposes of today's visit is to accompany John to the Manchester

Eric Randerson trying out another Rovers marketing idea ...
(Photo from Sheffield Newspapers).

United v. Barcelona European Cup game. Glynn has played at Old Trafford on numerous occasions, while I was in the Rochdale team, which met Manchester United in the third round of the F.A. Cup in 1986. That was in front of a crowd of 45,000. One of John's friends, Harold Shapiro, a very amusing Scottish doctor, joins us as a late replacement for Ian.

We chat about a variety of subjects, while Glynn preens himself in a bathroom adjoining John's office. Eventually, he re-emerges, not looking much different than when he began, though he does smell sweeter. We leave in John's Bentley, with Glynn, the 'Doc' (as Glynn calls him) and myself squeezing into the back. Our driver tonight is Gareth who, apparently, I have played rugby against. Later, we are to meet and discuss an offer with John Sheridan. We enjoy a very nice meal in the dinning area at Old Trafford and when John Sheridan has still not appeared, John searches for him. After a while, J. Sheridan appears and then we wait for John Ryan to return.

Once we're in our seats, and the game has started, Glynn and myself admire the technical aspects of each player's touch. Ryan Giggs destroys the Barcelona full-back Luis Henrique and Beckham produces one of his amazing free kicks. The second half contrasts with the first, Barcelona outplaying United, the game ending 3-3. Luis Henrique moved to mid-field and was world class. For United, this is probably not a good result, yet it was a thoroughly exciting contest.

Leaving the ground, we make our way to Hale and Marcello's, joining a few more people.

I leave around midnight.

Thursday 17 September

I enjoy the luxury of getting up later than normal, attending a business luncheon at Manchester City, and being introduced to some of John's business colleagues. Whilst having played at Maine Road, I have never been inside their hospitality suite, which is very nice. The food is better than at Old Trafford and my wine glass never seems to be empty. Johnny Giles, the former Leeds United hero, is the guest speaker and, after listening to him, I spend time conversing about database marketing. Some might feel this is esoteric, though I feel strongly that it is under-used in professional sport.

Friday 18 September

A delayed start to the day due to an upset stomach which has lingered from the previous evening. Eventually, I arrive in Doncaster for an appointment with a PFA representative. We want to recruit players on YTS and scholarship programmes. They seem reluctant to allow this for a number of reasons, including previous problems with Dinard and the fact that we are in the Conference. In my opinion, the Conference seems to be the league that nobody wants. This is a pity because it contains some good teams like Woking, Yeovil, Stevenage Cheltenham, Rushden and Diamonds, and even Doncaster Rovers.

Bad news. Our new kit from Asics has not arrived yet. Hopefully, it will be here in time for tomorrow's game. But, I have my doubts.

Saturday 19 September

On the way to Doncaster, I ponder on today's home game opponents – Rushden and Diamonds, from the Northampton area. The club is owned by Max Griggs, reputedly worth over £300m, generated by his company Dr Martens. M. Griggs was formerly a Northampton Town director but, several years ago, merged two amateur teams to create Rushden and Diamonds. They are now sitting at the top of the Conference, having lost only one of their last ten games. With a new stadium and a full-time squad of 28 players and 14 YTS lads, they are, in many ways, light years ahead, compared to ourselves and a number of other clubs.

Today sees the opening of the newly refurbished bars, in the main stand, badly damaged in the 1995 fire. John Ryan very kindly provided finance for the refit to be carried out. On arriving at the ground, I tour round the bars with Alick Jeffrey Jnr who has co-ordinated much of the work. The bars look great and should generate some much-needed revenue for the Club. Gazing out of the windows, I notice the Rushden and Diamonds team arriving in a luxurious coach, which they probably own. Like money bags Manchester United, I suspect they are the team everybody wants to beat. And, when the players step down from the coach, they seemingly display a smug arrogance. It must be nice for them being in a comfortable situation, worrying about nothing else only playing football. By comparison, we are still along way off from achieving this. I genuinely believe the new Doncaster Rovers will emerge around December/January. Until then, we have to do the best we can, under difficult conditions.

There's a great atmosphere around the ground, with lots of children in the crowd, which is an added bonus. Hopefully, they will continue to support the team for many years to come.

In the Board Room, I chat with Max Griggs and his fellow directors. I note they are well organised, having many media/press people here reporting on the game. Before taking my seat in the stand, I nip into our dressing room, wishing the players good luck. Whilst I've

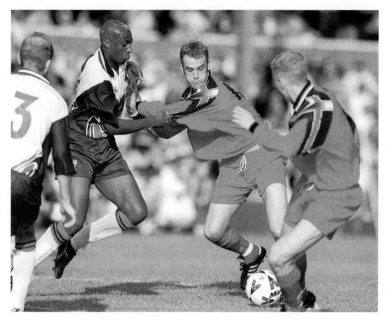

Rovers forward, Mark Hulme, holds off a challenge (Photo by Shaun Flannery).

really no idea what to expect in the game ahead, I'm delighted to hear there are over 3,000 people in attendance. This is quite fantastic. Rushden's players are probably the tallest I have seen this season in the Conference and definitely the most physical. In a game with a team like this, Ian Snodin ought to have been playing, though injury has ruled him out for a few weeks. We give a creditable first half performance and it ends all square at 0-0, with plenty of commitment being shown by both sides.

The second half begins in a similar fashion and, before long, our fans are screaming for a foul by the Rushden keeper on Dino. The keeper also handles the ball outside the penalty area. To everybody's amazement – even the Rushden directors – the referee waves play on. Seconds later, the away team score.

John Ryan leaps to his feet screaming in protest at the previous incident. And, while at football matches I tend to keep my emotions under control, there was not a more blatant foul or a handball than those just seen. It is definitely going to be a long season. With ten minutes to go, the game is slipping away from us. Ian Snodin plays his final card – sending on centre half Mark Hume to play up front. Well, we have nothing to lose. Everyone anxiously studies their watches. The 90th minute passes, then the 91st and 92nd. How much longer can this torture go on? At the very least, we deserved a draw. The referee puts the whistle to his mouth as we begin our last attack.

'He's bloody done it,' I scream, seeing big Barnsley lad Mark Hume, score the equaliser.

American College students at Belle Vue (Photo by Paul Gilligan).

The crowd and our players go absolutely mental. No sooner have Rushden kicked off from the centre circle than the referee blows for full time. At least he gets that right. The Doncaster gladiators are applauded from the field, while the referee receives a police escort to the dressing room. The Doncaster fans are very upset by his afternoon's performance. Even Paul May whose knowledge of football is limited thought 'the referee had a shocker.'

Realistically, I suppose we are content with a draw, the man-of-the-match award going to our player Kevin McIntyre. He was absolutely magnificent. I have not seen a better example of an attacking full back/wing back for a long time. Let's hope we can get him to sign a contract.

I have a quick chat with our coaches and then make my way up to the new bars. It's good to see they are packed out. At 7.00 pm, it's time to go home.

Monday 21 September

Great news. The kit, which was promised for the Rushden game, has finally turned up. Our lads should be able to wear it for tomorrow's game against Morecambe.

Today also sees the start of our new commercial manager, Nigel Reed. I like his enthusiasm and he has both the experience and the ideas to do well. Joining forces with Alick Jeffrey Jnr, who will be his assistant, should provide us with a winning combination to encourage sponsorship. It is something we desperately need because, normally, sports clubs have a whole list of sponsors. We have none. During the previous regime's

'Dino' Maamria (Photo by Shaun Flannery).

last year of control, a campaign was launched, encouraging companies not to be involved with the Club. I'm sure the intentions were well founded, only it has certainly made life difficult for those following on.

The stresses and strains of the job are eased, to some extent, a little later in the day when Alick Jnr, Nigel and myself are guests of Graham Rhoden at his hotel, the Earl of Doncaster. I have the largest prawn and avocado sandwich I have ever had and, together, we work out a deal. We get free accommodation whenever required, in return for the hotel being offered free advertising. I also book three sportsman's dinners at the hotel, showing some commitment, on our part, to the new partnership.

September 1998

Bad news greets me when I return to the ground. Ian Snodin says he has just been in conversation with Kevin Sheedy at Tranmere, regarding Kevin McIntyre. Rushden and Diamonds have offered £10,000 for him. Needless to say, Ian and myself are unimpressed. A player, who was available to us on a free transfer, will now cost £10,000.

Tuesday 22 September

Today, representatives from the Football League are assessing the ground, to decide whether we warrant an A, B or C grading. An A would ensure that no more improvements were required for a couple of years. Getting a B or a C would indicate more work was necessary. Considering that over £40,000 has already been spent, we don't really want to incur any further expense.

After driving through thick fog and swirling rain on the 'tops', I arrive at the ground checking that tea coffee and sandwiches are being provided in the Board Room in readiness for our

Kevin McIntyre side-steps a tackle (Photo by Shaun Flannery).

guests. As they appear, I am called to answer an urgent 'phone call from the chairman. Eventually, I return to be greeted by officers from Doncaster Council, including John McLoughlin; Jack Crawford and Chris Walley from the Football League; Geoff Wilson, Football Licensing Authority; and Albert Paget, our safety officer/stadium manager.

Those on our side, easily answer questions thrown at them by the Football League, and then their representatives inspect the ground, being quite impressed by the work and progress carried out thus far. Twenty minutes later and we've got an A grading, providing one or two further small improvements are made. This means that if, over the next few seasons, we manage to win promotion from the Conference, we can take our rightful place back in the League, without any questions being raised over the suitability of our ground.

The afternoon goes well, with Ian Snodin presenting me with a 'manager's coat from our kit sponsors Asics. This should keep me warm during tonight's game at Morecambe. Additionally, Asics have sent our away strip, which I had a hand in designing. Whilst I'm no Jean Paul Gaultier, it looks OK. Alas, they haven't sent any socks. So, I give permission for someone to buy 20 pairs, enabling us to wear the new away kit tonight. Such decisions!

I leave for Morecambe at 4.30 pm, picking up a friend in Oldham. Steve Nicol is meeting me at the game, where he will sign a contract, joining us for 18 months. During this time, it is hoped, he will add more stability to the squad.

On arrival at Morecambe's ground, we immediately seek the Board Room comforts. I am also meeting Ian Green, another Westferry director. He is on business in the north west and has found time to attend the game. He is probably one of the happiest men I have ever met, his face always painted with a smile.

Two hours later, everyone from Doncaster is celebrating a 2-1 victory, Glenn Kirkwood and Mark Hume (now playing up-front), scoring the goals. For us, an away win, has been a long time coming and, tonight, it was thoroughly deserved. To put the 'cherry on top of the cake,' I have also secured Steve Nicol's signature on a contract.

Wednesday 23 September

Today, the Club's directors and myself, should have been in London, for a meeting with the F.A., only we cancelled the appointment, due to previous commitments. Lunch time is taken up with negotiations involving the chairman and Paul May. Eventually, Ian Snodin joins us and we talk about our present position and the search for players.

Everyone is delighted with how the Club is progressing both on and off the field. We are playing great football and have been unlucky not to win more games. Hopefully, this will change once Ian can stabilize the squad. It is also stated that money is very tight and will have to be spent wisely. Particular attention is to be paid to maintaining a steady cash flow.

P.M.: 'I think it is amazing how the fans have backed the club.'

J.R.: 'Yes, and once the team is regularly winning games, crowds will flock to the ground. Doncaster is a larger area than Blackburn, Barnsley and Oldham, and they've all had teams in the Premiership.'

I.M.: 'Our problem is, we have no more money available to buy players and meet their various signing-on fees and wage demands.'

J.R.: 'I will do all I can to make finance available for new players. My heart would break seeing Rovers drop down another division.'

September 1998

Thursday 24 September

Travelling through the early morning rush hour traffic, I am longing to attend the merchandise exhibition at the G-Mex in Manchester. Off-field activities are a major source of revenue, desperately needed to boost a club's finances. Normally, I go to one or two exhibitions per year, picking up ideas or contacts. Today, alas, I cannot be there, mainly due to an appointment with Doncaster Council Leader Malcolm Glover. I'm putting ideas to him for community and youth involvement with Rovers. M. Glover seems a nice man and, it transpires, there is a lot of 'common ground' during our discussions. Later, we decide to issue a Press release, letting the general public know the Club's plans for the future. I agree to have meetings with M. Glover on a regular basis, and take names of contacts, within the council, who may be able help us.

Back at the ground, Nigel Reed, Alick Jeffrey Jnr, and myself talk about the newly formed commercial and marketing department. I have booked three sportsman's dinners at the Earl of Doncaster Hotel, one before Christmas and two in the New Year. The first one is to be held on 29 October and 'there's plenty of time to sell it out' is the instruction I give to them both.

During the afternoon there are more negotiations with the PFA regarding YTS players and the new scholarships, both of which we desperately need. The PFA and FA provide the finances for the establishment of schools of excellence and YTS. As a Conference side we are not entitled to any of it, a situation I will not let go unchallenged. The PFA say they may 'at some stage, allow us to have YTS players, although not funded.'

Clubs don't realise that once relegated from the league, they are entitled to nothing. This is ironic as a lot of Conference clubs are better organised than many of those in the third or even second divisions. Yet, we are not deemed as worthy of support to set up and run centres of excellence.

Furthermore, we appear to have more working parties than are necessary, supposedly studying Ajax and other clubs who have successfully developed their own players. This has led to European funding which is being passed on to British clubs in order to develop local talent. However, even though Doncaster Rovers were in the league for years, we are not entitled to a bean. What a load of bollocks!

Another meeting with the supporters club and then I drive back over the hills.

Friday 25 September

To gather further information about previous local YTS, and how they were funded, I visit a local school, once involved with them. Two hours later, I'm none the wiser. The school insists that after being given verbal assurances over receiving £8,000-£10,000, no funding was forthcoming. On leaving, I conclude that the YTS situation is a mess. Very little paper work exists to accurately assess what has happened and, it will be a nightmare unravelling it all.

I arrive back at the ground to be greeted by a another crisis. The local coach company that we use have sent only a basic vehicle for the gruelling trip to Yeovil. The players are making the journey today while the chairman and myself, too busy to do the same, plan to fly there by helicopter tomorrow, weather permitting. On taking a closer look at the coach, I feel that some local people and companies enjoy taking the mickey out of us. No way will the coach company receive full payment from us for sending this vehicle. Someone has to make a stand, and it looks like it will be me on this occasion.

Everybody takes and nobody gives.

Saturday 26 September

Bad weather means that the helicopter cannot take off. What a disappointment.

The afternoon is not wasted. I have a game of rugby with the Oldham rugby union veterans' team, playing at full back. Even though I am only 33, I qualify as a 'vet', due to my body being knackered. After the game, which we lose, I feel very sore. I hobble upstairs, at the club house, still wearing my kit and covered from head to toe in mud, searching through the 'latest scores' on teletext, to see how Rovers are doing.

It's 2-0 to us. I run downstairs, telling my team mates. After all, they do take the mickey out of my chosen profession, particularly as I'm working for Doncaster Rovers. I take a quick shower then sprint up to the bar, seeing the teleprinter spewing out the football results – Yeovil 2-Doncaster Rovers 2.

'I don't believe it, I don't believe it,' I proclaim, in my worst Victor Meldrew voice.

Two nil up and we only draw. Well, I suppose it was better than losing, and Yeovil are formidable opponents.

Monday 28 September

An early morning chat with our scout in Ireland who, a while ago, offered a winger to us. Unfortunately, the player has pulled a hamstring and will be out of action for a few weeks. I am keen to develop strong links with Ireland where, at some stage, I hope to create a mini-Doncaster Rovers team. Whilst I know itís a grand scheme, we have to develop our own talent, particularly when considering the situation over here with wages, transfer fees and the Bosman ruling.

The rest of the day is eaten away, chewing over fund-raising schemes.

Tuesday 29 September

A short time is taken paper pushing, then I drive to Notts County's ground, attending an FA seminar about sponsorship. I may not learn anything new but, given the Club's present financial predicament, I need to explore every possibility.

Wednesday 30 September

Finally, my hire car goes back tomorrow and my new, lease car is being delivered. I stay overnight at the Earl of Doncaster.

October 1998

Thursday 1 October

An early start, waiting for the lease car to arrive at Belle Vue. The 'delivery' driver takes me out to have a look at it – a Ford Granada Scorpio. The colour is silver blue, and I imagine Connor saying it's the same shade as the Man. City strip. I have a little drive round the car park, after inspecting both the interior, and exterior, features. It has an automatic gearbox, making my long journeys a little more bearable. It's roomy too, providing much-needed comfort for my bulky frame. And, there's an impressive stereo, which will be well used in the months ahead. After pronouncing that everything is in order, a form is signed, and the driver is directed to the railway station to make his homeward journey.

A little later, Ian and Glynn's vehicles arrive from Dixon Rover, a local dealership, based in Kirk Sandall. Their cars are being sponsored, as opposed to mine which is on lease. Several dealers decided that I travel too many miles, to qualify for a 'sponsored' vehicle.

The kit replicas arrive from Asics. These, and other items, will be sold from a porta-cabin – the club's shop – adjacent to the ground.

Kevin Phelan, Aiden Phelan (they are still not related) and Paul May arrive for a progress report. Aiden Phelan buys some replica kits for his kids. He is delighted at how the Club is progressing, and feels the staff have done a remarkable job.

Friday 2 October

A meeting at the Yorkshire Residential School for the Deaf, situated a short distance from Belle Vue. We are using their sports facilities in exchange for us allocating their students free match-day tickets. One of the topics on the agenda is basketball. They want to know if a basket ball arena can be accommodated in the new football stadium. Unfortunately, the answer is no. I say unfortunate, because it comes second in my list of favourite sports. I am a great advocate of the game, being a fan of the Chicago Bulls, and Michael Jordan. I have studied basketball in detail, and believe the NBA has done well to transform the sport, and the various clubs. In the 1970s, basketball was regarded as a poor sport, with no real spectator appeal. After a great deal of effort and marketing, it has become, arguably, the number one sport, with many clubs and players being household names, world-wide.

The Club shop is fitted out, and is beginning to look attractive, with the replica kits on display.

We sign Andy Hayward on loan from Hednesford Town. He's a former Rotherham United player.

Saturday 3 October

We have a home game against Farnborough Town.

It's a bright sunny afternoon for one of the most one-sided games I've ever seen, Rovers playing extremely well. If this had been a boxing match, it would have been stopped, long before the final bell only, once again, we lose 2-1, Colin Sutherland scoring our goal. Whilst Rovers goalkeeper, Woods, had been outstanding in the previous three games, Neville Southall returned today, and he gave a poor performance. I take consolation, believing that we will not reach our peak until after Christmas.

There was a crowd of 3, 468, made up of about 25 from Farnborough.

Jamie Barnwell-Edinboro, winning the ball,
against Farnborough
(Photo by Shaun Flannery).

In the Board Room, our quests include Council Leader Malcolm Glover, Doncaster Central Labour MP Rosie Winterton, and the producer of Jeremy Clarkson's Top Gear show, with whom I discuss details of filming around Belle Vue.

We have a great day in the Club shop, with over £4,000 being taken, mainly from the sale of replica shirts.

On the way home, my thoughts wonder back to this afternoon's game, concluding I've watched some of the best football I've seen us play for some time. Many teams, encountered this season, have admitted we are the best footballing side they have played against. But, that is usually said after they have beaten us … Just wait until the New Year. I am sure we will achieve or win something.

Monday 5 October

Travelling in the new vehicle makes my journey a lot easier. After the defeat on Saturday, we are bottom of the league. On arrival at the ground, I join in a discussion with the Snodins, who are holding a post-mortem on the game. We all agree that the football was outstanding, but the result went against us.

I have a brief word with Nigel and Alick, learning there is continuing interest in the commercial department, with more and more sponsors eager to become involved with the Club. We discuss our merchandise. I have an idea for producing a strip from an earlier period, probably the 1960s. This could be sponsored by businessmen wanting to recall the Club's happier times. They might even tell their kids 'how painful it was to head footballs in those days', and 'how newspapers were pushed down socks for shin pads.'

Today, the draw for the 3rd Qualifying Round of the FA Cup is made. This is un-chartered territory for us, having just come out of the Football League. At least we have a home draw against Flixton, from the Manchester area, and it is a game we are expected to win. But, in the FA Cup, who can predict the outcome?

Tuesday 6 October

A visit to a number of companies in Leicester who may be able to supply clothing for the Club shop. Hopefully, one day, we will create our own brand of merchandise. It is definitely the way forward for lower-league clubs. The mark-up on goods by manufacturers is too high, having to pass this expense on to customers. If quality and prices can be closely controlled, the goods will become more attractive.

Wednesday 7 October

My birthday, I'm 34, and it's also my wedding anniversary.

October 1998

Tommy Wright signs a two-year contract. Terms are also negotiated with John Sheridan, playing for us on a match-to-match basis. I fear we cannot meet his expectations.

Alick, Nigel and myself talk about the previous evening's fund-raising event at the Clay Lane Social Club, where a comedian and a band performed. It seems to have gone well, several hundred pounds being added to the Club's coffers.

As it's my birthday, I celebrate with the staff, providing a number of cream cakes. I don't have any, as I don't eat cream. On the way home, I buy two bunches of flowers – such decadence – for my wife, acknowledging our wedding anniversary. Later, we have a glass of wine together, and I open a few more birthday cards. All of them tell me how old, senile and fat I'm becoming. And, these are from my friends.

Thursday 8 October

I'm asked to organise refreshments in the Board Room as talks are taking place over the projected new stadium. As this event largely concerns the architects, and will deal with technical aspects of the project, I do not attend.

Friday 9 October

Paul May visits for one of our regular finance meetings.

Stewart Rose shows me a range of sports merchandise. I've dealt with him before. He usually has the right product, with the right quality, at the right price.

An approach is made by a Doncaster Schools organisation, asking if they can play some games at Belle View. I agree, as it seems a good idea.

The papers are awash with a story, claiming that Neville Southall has played his last game for Doncaster Rovers. As may have been predicted, Ian is not very happy.

Whilst it does appear that his time with us is over, nobody can deny his career has been outstanding. In the meantime, we have secured goalkeeper Andy Woods until the end of the season. He arrived from Halifax some weeks ago, to cover while Neville was injured. Another former Halifax player, Ian Duerden, has also signed a contract today.

Saturday 10 October

We play Woking at home today. We lose 1-0, their keeper playing an outstanding game. We had a lot of chances only failed to score. They had two, and made one of them count. Whilst the underlying factor, in all our recent games, is that we are playing well, we are not scoring goals. The gate is 2,833, our lowest to date this season, though a marked improvement on the past few years' attendances.

England play Bulgaria in the European Championships, drawing 0-0.

I drive home, thoroughly disappointed with our result. Hopefully, a good run in the FA Cup or the Endsleigh League Trophy, will lift our spirits.

Monday 12 October

Gazza makes the headlines in many of the morning papers – for his drinking prowess. This deflects somewhat from England's disappointing draw with Bulgaria.

I speak to Mickey Burns from the PFA, regarding the establishment of a YTS at Doncaster. Taking into account the Club's previously difficulties in maintaining the scheme, not least the question of finance, he suggests a way forward.

We sign another young player, Matthew Caudwell, from Hallam F.C. near Sheffield. I learn that Ian and Glynn are impressed with him in training. He looks about 12 years old, though I am reliably informed that he is 21. Little by little, Ian is slowly putting together a great squad of players and, a bonus is, they are mostly young lads.

Tuesday 13 October

We are still bottom of the league. I don't like this, and I keep telling myself there is no need to panic. We will turn things around after Christmas.

Matt Caudwell (Photo by Shaun Flannery).

Wednesday 14 October

I talk with Dave Parker about establishing an official Doncaster Rovers internet site. There are several unofficial sites operating. Unfortunately, these do not reflect a true picture of what is happening at the Club, although some are quite good.

Chester City, in the 3rd Division, are experiencing acute financial problems. This prompts several questions in the minds of those concerned with Doncaster Rovers. If Chester fold, can we go back into the league? Is it an issue we could legally challenge? Another option considered is that of buying Chester City F.C. and somehow replacing them in the league. We check the FA handbook, and have several high-ranking discussions, only to discover that their demise would not open a back door for us back into the league.

Nevertheless, things are looking up on the commercial side. We strike a deal with local firms The Tile Depot, and Charlesworths, who will pay £5,000 each, to place large advertising boards on the front of the stand. Although to some clubs this would seem a small amount, it is a welcome cash injection for us, and is much appreciated.

Additionally, Alick Jeffrey Jnr and myself have a meeting with John Fairhurst, a former Rovers player from the 1960s, who now holds a senior position at Polypipe, a large PLC, with offices near the town centre. John has intimated that Polypipe may wish to be involved in some way with the Club, so we will explore a number of options with him.

On my return to Belle Vue, I am informed the police will be charging us for their attendance at the Flixton fixture. That's amazing, particularly as the away side will only bring between 50-100 fans with them.

Thursday 15 October

We are drawn against Avesta in the Sheffield & Hallamshire Cup. It comes as a surprise as we didn't realise we were in this competition, and it does not include any professional sides other than ourselves. Ian Snodin is extremely frustrated by the news, mentioning we will have to cancel Conference fixtures to play in the games. I decide to speak to the Conference about the situation. They say it will cost us £500 to withdraw from the competition.

During the evening, Ian and myself are guests of *Doncaster Star*, at a dinner held at Doncaster Golf Club. Malcolm Lord, a well-known compare, is present, and his eyes light up when I appear, realising that poking fun at me will provide him with another 20 minutes of material. I feel the night out is a welcome break for Ian, who spends many hours watching football matches each week, in the hope of finding new players to bring to the Club.

Friday 16 October

Paul May, John Ryan and Kevin Phelan are gathering at the Club during the morning, talking about the new stadium, and Ian and Glynn's contracts.

I am asked if Flixton can send some turnstile 'checkers' for the game tomorrow. I politely tell them to 'get stuffed', though mention officials from the club are welcome to inspect our computer system, recording attendance figures.

A letter from the FA insists that we attend a meeting with its representatives on the 21st to explain the current situation, regarding ownership, at the Club.

In the afternoon, John Ryan and myself talk with a player, Andy Saville, at the Grand St Leger Hotel. He lives in Doncaster, travelling each week to play with Cardiff City. He thinks he is available on a free transfer, so we have a good chat and make him an offer. He agrees to come back to us.

The evening is taken up with John Ryan, Ian, Glynn, and myself attending a Doncaster Rovers supporters club meeting. A variety of subjects are aired, including the supporters club's desire to sell their own merchandise. This proves to be a contentious issue, and we agree to disagree on certain points. We do agree however, to them selling selected items in their own shop at Belle Vue, providing it is not confused with official Doncaster Rovers merchandise.

Saturday 17 October

It's raining, and I'm not expecting a large crowd, as this cup match with Flixton will not fire the imagination of locals. We win comfortably, 2-0, the main excitement coming at the end of the game, from a small gas leak in the boiler house, under the main stand. As a matter of safety, we evacuate the Board Room and dressing rooms. The problem is soon solved.

No checkers came from Flixton, though their secretary examined our computer system. The attendance figure was around 2,500, from which, Flixton will receive half the proceeds, once expenses are deducted.

I drive home believing a decent run in the FA or Endsleigh Cup, could capture the imagination of supporters, though our main priority is survival.

Monday 19 October

Ian Snodin talks to Tranmere Rovers about signing Kevin McIntyre on a permanent contract. The price on his head has now risen to £50,000. Initially, he was available on a free transfer. I find it amazing that, after a few games with Doncaster Rovers, he now commands this kind of figure. We decline the offer.

John Ryan talks with Westferry about purchasing the 'football side' of the Club. A deal in principle is agreed, though this may take several months to complete. It was always Westferry's intention to sell this part of the Club, and an offer has appeared quicker than envisaged. Westferry, in the meantime, will still hold on to the Belle Vue lease, and try to make progress in securing a deal for a new stadium. John has made the move for the 'football side', because he is a fanatical fan and is concerned about our league position. In his present position, being a non-executive director, there is not much he can do, until he owns the football side. It is a position he fully understands.

In the FA Trophy Cup-a non-league competition, we draw Frickley Athletic. Reaching the final, played at Wembley, would be great for us though, I feel, as a team, we are not quite at our best just yet.

A 'live' interview on Radio Sheffield on the ups and downs so far this season. I've talked live on radio many times before, though I've never actually heard myself. Seemingly, I must make some sense, as they keep inviting me.

Tuesday 20 October

I hear that John Sheridan has signed for Oldham Athletic, presumably for the figure he put to us, but which was beyond our means. We wish him well.

October 1998

I stay the night in Doncaster, in readiness for travelling to London for the appointment with the FA.

Wednesday 21 October

On arriving at Kings Cross, I can't help but feel sympathy for the victims who perished in the horrendous fire, which engulfed the area.

I travel on three different 'Tube' lines before reaching Lancaster Gate. The meeting is not at the FA's headquarters, due to repairs still being carried out following fire damage, but a short distance away, at the Royal Merchant Navy Hotel, which takes some finding. I turn up, a quarter-of-an-hour before the allotted time of 11.45 am, though I'm kept waiting a further 35 minutes. In the meantime, I have a coffee, run my eyes over the hotel decor and people watch. As the hotel's name may have suggested, there are a few model ships dotted here and there, and couple of Uncle Albert (from Only Fools and Horses) look-alikes, frequenting the bar.

Eventually, I am called and, after introducing themselves, the 12-strong FA committee, bombard me with questions: Who am I? Who are Westferry? Why are they based in Ireland? Who is John Ryan? Who is Paul May?

They also ask details about Ken Richardson, still awaiting trial over the Belle Vue fire.

I answer each question as best as I can, but I am sweating. No conclusions are reached, and at the end of the meeting they thank me for my attendance. On the journey home, I run through the grilling I received. It is not an experience I would want to endure again, not on my own anyway.

I am back in Doncaster around two hours later, the town being conveniently situated on the rail network.

Thursday 22 October

An early morning appointment at Manchester University, regarding my assignment in Sport Law. Reluctantly, I defer this until next year.

John Ryan is in Dublin for a meeting with Westferry.

On reaching Doncaster, I prepare some figures to talk over with Paul May. Unfortunately, this is cancelled due to his car breaking down on the way to Doncaster.

Friday 23 October

A conversation with John Moules at the Conference offices, about the ongoing saga with Avesta, the team we are to play in the Sheffield & Hallamshire Cup. Everyone seems to be insisting that we play the tie. Normally, I would not be too concerned, but as we only have a small squad, I don't want to risk players being injured. Our main priority this year is to survive in the Conference.

John Ryan informs me about the meeting in Ireland – things are progressing nicely. He gives me directions to his new house, as I will see him there tomorrow, before we travel to the Cheltenham match. I hope he does not have the same trouble with this property as he did the other one.

We have decided to place a bid of £10,000 for Kevin McIntyre. It will be our final one. Again, the deal is to be financed by John Ryan.

The cheques arrive from Charlesworths and The Tile Depot, giving a much-needed boost to our cash flow.

I finish at 6 pm.

Up the Rovers (Photo by Shaun Flannery).

Saturday 24 October

After taking numerous wrong turnings, I eventually find John's house. A little later, we are heading southwards, for the clash with Cheltenham who are the new favourites to win the Conference. I'm at the wheel of his Bentley and, as usual, we discuss aspects of the Rovers team, besides trying to predict the result. It's pouring with rain outside, whilst the radio informs that games are being called off. I 'phone Cheltenham, being told everything should be OK. Obviously, someone has ordered extra pies, which will be wasted if the game is postponed. We drive through Cheltenham, John reminiscing that he once lived here for a short period.

We arrive at the ground and I announce 'Chairman of Doncaster Rovers Football Club' to the car park attendant – forgetting to add that John is sitting in the passenger seat. While making our way to the Board Room, I learn the referee has not arrived, and there is some concern over the pitch's condition. Outside, I notice the rain is becoming more persistent, and I aim to make my own assessment. But, I decide against walking on the pitch, at the last moment, not wanting to ruin my shoes. I'm convinced however, that it's 'playable'. The linesmen have arrived, and they agree with me, though the Cheltenham manager does not. I phone Ian Snodin, with the players on the coach, expressing my concern that the game might be called off. They have just left the hotel, after having a pre-match meal. I tell him to get here as quickly as possible as, I feel, in his absence, the 'home' manager may influence any decisions taken. When Ian arrives, he inspects the pitch for himself, declaring it playable. The referee has telephoned, saying he will arrive shortly, being marooned in traffic. In the meantime, the linesmen announce the game is on.

Today provides an opportunity to test ourselves against the best opponents in the Conference. But, a strange decision by the referee unsettles the team. About six yards out from our goal, the ball hits Doncaster defender Scott Maxfield in the face. The referee awards Cheltenham a penalty and sends off Scott for deliberate hand ball. Scott leaves the field, his face still red from where the ball hit him. Eventually, we draw level through a Mark Hulme goal, only for them to snatch a late winner.

Afterwards, I bump into Cheltenham manager Steve Cotterill, and reintroduce myself. In 1986, we were together at Farnham Park rehabilitation centre, near Slough. I was receiving treatment to rescue my playing career, while he was there recovering from a knee injury. Eventually, he went on to play for Wimbledon and Bournemouth. He is currently regarded as one of the best young managers around.

Monday 26 October

We feel close to securing a deal with Kevin McIntyre, if we can agree personal terms.

Paul May arrives and, yes we can meet these, only after the £10,000 asking price has been paid into our account by John Ryan.

Tuesday 27 October

Reluctantly, Kevin McIntyre has decided to stay at Tranmere.

We finally manage to finish the necessary work to acquire a safety certificate, stating all the ground's electrical equipment is OK.

I discuss with Alick and Nigel, Thursday evening's sportsman's dinner, and fine tune the details.

I leave Doncaster early, picking up Connor, as we're due at Old Trafford to watch Man. Utd. play Bury in the Worthington Cup. During the pre-match meal, Connor enjoys chicken nuggets, and manages to get Phil Neville's autograph. Phil is out tonight, and the United team is not at full strength.

As with most clubs, who come to Old Trafford, Bury try to restrict United's scoring opportunities. It turns out to be a dour game in front of sizeable, but not a capacity, crowd. Connor remarks that he's bored and the game drifts into extra time. We leave

Jodie and Tracey show off Rovers' merchandise in the Club shop
(Photo from Sheffield Newspapers).

early, avoiding the inevitable traffic jams. On our way home, I turn on the radio, learning United have scored two goals. By this time, Connor has fallen asleep.

Wednesday 28 October

I converse with Mike Fowler from Doncaster College. He wants to make a video, charting the Club's progress this season. It seems a good idea, and has my blessing, subject to me approving the end product, before going on sale.

Thursday 29 October

The morning is passed catching up on paper work, becoming mountainous. Why is it that football clubs seemingly generate reams and reams of paper?

The remainder of the day is taken up in the shop, making sure the merchandise is ordered in time for Christmas.

Paul May attends this evening's sportsman's dinner at the Earl with a friend who is 'Bilko's' double. Compare Malcolm Lord has noticed the resemblance too, pulling his leg mercilessly. That is, after he has shifted his attention from Ian Snodin. I retire to bed very late, staying overnight in the hotel.

October/November 1998

Friday 30 October

I meet Paul May at breakfast, only to discover that 'Bilko' has left early. Paul reveals that he looked 'rough' but admitted he'd had a good evening. I arrive at the ground, closing each door quietly behind me, sensing that any loud noise may detonate an explosion in my head. I wander into the commercial department, congratulating Nigel and Alick on organising a successful evening's entertainment. It is good to see them in a worse condition that myself.

During the day, the Avesta problem raises its head again and, in a last ditch attempt to get us out of the competition, I telephone Peter Hunter at the Conference. He will see what he can do.

Late in the afternoon, 'Bilko' phones to say that he had a good evening.

Saturday 31 October

Today, it's Guiseley, at home, in the 4th Qualifying Round of the FA Cup. A good crowd of 2,495 sees us win 3-1, with Ian Duerden, looking a useful acquisition, scoring two goals. The next stage of the competition, the First Round proper, will see some of the football league clubs entering the fray, with the draw being made live on SKY Television.

We draw Southend, away.

Monday 2 November

Whilst on holiday in America, John Ryan 'phones, quizzing me about the Guiseley game. I provide him with full details.

Later, the interviews are arranged for the book-keeper/financial controller post.

Two players are told that we are terminating their contracts, by mutual consent.

FOOTBALL CONFERENCE
(up to and including Oct. 26)

	P	W	D	L	F	A	Pts
Cheltenham T.	15	9	5	1	33	16	32
Rushden & D.	14	9	3	2	32	12	30
Stevenage Boro.	16	8	5	3	21	14	29
Kingstonian	15	8	3	4	25	21	27
Hayes	14	8	2	4	19	18	26
Kettering T.	15	7	4	4	19	12	25
Hednesford T.	14	6	5	3	19	16	23
Hereford Utd.	14	6	4	4	18	14	22
Kidderminster H.	15	6	3	6	23	18	21
Yeovil Town	15	5	6	4	21	20	21
Southport	14	5	4	5	21	21	19
Northwich V.	15	5	4	6	15	17	19
Dover Ath.	13	4	6	3	13	14	18
Telford Utd.	14	4	5	5	14	19	17
Morecambe	15	5	2	8	21	32	17
Leek Town	14	5	0	9	21	19	15
Forest Green R.	14	3	5	6	16	20	14
Welling Utd.	16	2	8	6	15	23	14
Woking	14	3	4	7	17	21	13
Farnborough T.	14	3	3	8	16	29	12
Barrow	15	2	5	8	15	30	11
ROVERS	15	2	4	9	14	22	10

Conference table, showing Rovers at the bottom of the pile.

Tuesday 3 November

I speak to Kevin Phelan, who is liaising with Doncaster Council on several matters, including the new stadium, and sorting out a number of problems lingering from the Richardson era.

All the merchandise for Christmas has been chosen and ordered.

The staff ask me if we are having a Christmas party. I tell them, I will be happy to attend, but I am not organising it.

The first team plays a 'behind closed doors' game with Rotherham United.

Late in the afternoon, I meet with the junior supporters club, suggesting how to raise the membership.

Tonight, one of my favourite bands Hootie and the Blowfish are playing in Nottingham – some 40-odd miles away. Whilst I consider going to see them, I decide it's too far to travel.

Alick Jeffrey Jnr has organised a fund-raising race night this evening.

Ignacio Linarus Ibarra ('Nacho')
(Photo by Shaun Flannery).

Wednesday 4 November

Throughout the morning, I catch up on some filing, barely being able to see over my desk top.

John Ryan 'phones about two players. One is a lad called Harper, originally available on a free transfer, though his club now wants £5,000 for him. Ian decides not to take him.

Meanwhile, a Spanish player, Ignacio Linarus Ibarra, registers with us. No doubt his name will provide nightmares for our match day commentator Ken Avis. Ian Snodin, immediately simplifies it to 'Nacho'.

Alick's race night raised over £500 and, apparently, a good night was had by all.

During the evening, there's a gathering of Rovers Independent Fans Association, at the Park Hotel, a short distance from Belle Vue. It is a good open, and frank, meeting and the association's members, comprising mainly younger fans, state that communication is improving between themselves and the Club.

Another late evening for me.

November 1998

Thursday 5 November

Interviews are held in the morning for the financial position. A list of six candidates includes men and women, ages ranging between 25-65. Disappointingly, nobody is really suitable. After discussing the situation with Paul May, we decide it will be easier to scrap the post and, for the time being at least, restructure the existing office staff.

Kevin and Aiden Phelan (still not related) are over from Ireland, meeting with P. Smith who has now taken over Doncaster Dragons Rugby Club.

On the football side, Aiden is pleased with the progress, and commitment, made so far.

Friday 6 November

We terminate David Esdaille's contract, and agree a settlement figure. He is not in Ian's plans, so it is better that he leaves the Club.

In the evening, Alick Jeffrey Jnr and myself are guests of Radio Hallam's at the Natalie Imbruglia concert at the Doncaster Dome. Outside, we see people queueing for Daniel O'Donnell tickets. In my opinion, they are mad.

The Dome's concert hall, resembles a set from Grease (the school gymnasium) and lacks atmosphere. After a while, I meet up with Mike Davies from the *Don. Star*, having a few drinks, before the concert starts. Although, Natalie Imbruglia, is not one of my all time favourite artistes, I am pleasantly surprised by her competent energetic performance.

Afterwards, I'm struck with the idea of staging concerts at Belle Vue, attracting a wide variety of artistes.

Saturday 7 November

We're playing Stevenage away, though I've decided not to go, seeing the two boys instead. At 1 pm, I take Connor to Oldham Athletic's home game with Manchester City. It's good observing Oldham's new signing John Sheridan, though I wish he was still with us. City thrash the home side, who look like they will struggle for the remainder of the season.

I'm unable to discover Rovers' result until reaching home. A search through the teletext reveals a 2-0 defeat. Later in the evening, I agree to drown my sorrows at a friend's barbecue.

Monday 9 November

Ian Snodin talks about the defeat at Stevenage. Unfortunately, it's the same old story. We outplayed the opposition, only didn't get a result.

Charles Walker, a supporters club member, shows me a newspaper article he has obtained from Stockport. It details an alleged proposal involving Ken Richardson/Mark Weaver in buying Cheadle Town F.C. He asks if Westferry are involved – as I am perceived by some individuals as being 'Westferry'. I find the incident reveals that a deep mistrust, of those in charge at the Club, still exists amongst a number of the fans. I categorically deny that Westferry are involved with any alleged take-over at Cheadle.

Tuesday 10 November

I attend a football merchandising exhibition in Manchester. It is poor, though one or two items are interesting, particularly the cups and mugs. I am keen to develop our own range of products, as soon as possible.

Back in Doncaster, during the afternoon, I discuss with Ian Snodin, Saturday's away tie with Southend in the 1st Round of the FA Cup. It is agreed that we will stay in Southend on Friday night, and details will be finalised a little later.

Wednesday 11 November

A drive to Hednesford Town for a gathering of officials from Conference clubs. Many items are discussed including centres of excellence, which the Conference is trying to encourage all clubs to establish. Details are also given about a new sponsor for the Conference league, as it has been without one since Vauxhall pulled out.

Thursday 12 November

The day starts early for a rendezvous with Paul May and John Ryan, going over figures and budgets. Chocolate biscuits are always available when these two are in town. Clearly, I need them to visit more often. Our meetings have a humorous as well as serious side. We also discuss the latest football news. Peter Schmichael has announced he is leaving Man. Utd, and Roy Evans has left Liverpool after 30 years. Arsenal have lost 5-0 at home to Chelsea. The talk drifts on to Rovers' scarves and sweatshirts. John Ryan eventually buys a scarf to drape across the back window of his Bentley.

Friday 13 November

Not an unlucky day for me as, my pay slip reveals a tax rebate. I plot ways of concealing this from my wife.

John Ryan, Ray Thomas and myself are travelling on the team coach to Southend. It will give John and me some time to go through the take-over details, as well as providing him with a unique insight into a professional footballer's life. Shortly before we leave, Colin Sutherland has not turned up. Several attempts to contact him prove futile, so we leave, a player short.

During the journey, John Ryan observes, first hand, the football card schools at work, as well as experiencing the good-natured banter, which goes on. Nobody is safe from ridicule. Even, the chairman himself, giving as good as he gets.

In the evening, Ray and myself are the last to bed, not before guessing how many goals we will win by, in tomorrow's game.

Once in my room, I break the seal on a mini-bar, moving the drinks to one side and eating the chocolate.

November 1998

Saturday 14 November

I'm woken early by a call on my mobile. It's Joan Oldale, passing on a message that Southend's pitch is to be inspected. I peer out of a window, observing that it's raining slightly. I find John and Ian and we discuss the situation. Eventually, John, Ray and myself order a taxi, and travel to the ground, gathering more information. We stroll on to the pitch, being amazed as we can't see any problem. I relay this information to Ian at the hotel. At that point, the referee arrives and, after scrutinizing the pitch himself, gives the go ahead. As there is no point in the three of us travelling back to the hotel, we are invited into the club's restaurant area, where coffee and biscuits are provided. We also have a frank discussion with the referee (from the Football League) about various matters, and this enables John Ryan to exorcise some frustrations about the men in black before the game starts.

Several hundred Doncaster fans have made the long trek south and, unbelievably, they are out-chanting the home fans. The atmosphere is fantastic, and an early goal by Dave Penney, makes us believe we can sneak through to the next round. Southend hit the bar, have a chance cleared off the line and, before the end of the game, their fans are calling for manager Alvin Martin to be sacked. The final result is a 1-0 win for us. The Snodin brothers leap into the air with joy. Our fans are still singing 10 minutes after the players have left the pitch. The gate receipts show that over 500 of them made up the 3,700 gate. On the trip home, we are full of expectations, because if we can get through the next round, we might be drawn against one of the 'big boys' in the 3rd round.

I left home, on the outskirts of Oldham, at 7 am on Friday, returning at 11pm on Saturday night.

Monday 16 November

A rep I met at the sports merchandising exhibition last week, arrives at 10 am, and I pick his brains, for my long-term plans of developing our own range of goods. This is something I will work on during the coming months.

Tuesday 17 November

Paul May and myself gather with John Ryan in Cheshire, chewing over the Club's financial situation. It will be several months before John takes control of the 'football side,' and one of the items mentioned is the signing of new players. It is pointed out that, if any additional players are signed, he will have to finance all the costs. To some extent, he has been doing this already, even though he only has a non-executive role as Club chairman. John accepts this point, obviously aware of the fact that we are still bottom of the Conference and, being a fanatical Rovers fan, wants to do as much as he can to alter the situation.

We continue our conversations over lunch, before I travel back, independently, to Doncaster. Tonight, we have a game with Barrow, and the match sponsors are Beazer Homes, a firm of nationally-known house builders. Encouragingly, it is looking like the company will be our shirt sponsors.

Glynn Snodin at an after school event (Photo from Sheffield Newspapers).

The Barrow team includes four very experienced players: Mike Marsh; Mark Seagraves, ex-Liverpool; Andy Mutch, who formed a formidable partnership with Steve Bull at Wolves; and Tony Parkes, ex-Spurs. It seems incredible that players of such quality are in a team struggling at the foot of the Conference.

In terms of cliches, the match, for us, is 'a six-pointer' and, on a very cold, damp, foggy evening, we scrape a 2-1 win, with goals from G. Kirkwood and 'Dino'. This is seen by a crowd of 2,617, our lowest gate of the season.

November 1998

Wednesday 18 November

In the Second Round of the FA Cup, we've been drawn against Rushden & Diamonds, and will have to re-arrange our league game with Morecambe. We want to play the game on 22 December to help our cash-flow over Christmas, but they don't. Unfortunately, we cannot force the issue.

Good news. Beazer homes have agreed to sponsor the Club in a two-year deal. Being associated with a company of their calibre gives us added credibility and, again, indicates we are developing.

I finalise details for the visit of Jeremy Clarkson and his entourage.

Jeremy Clarkson – a closet Rovers fan? (Photo from Sheffield Newspapers).

Thursday 19 November

On the way to work, there are traffic delays at Holmfirth. It's the fog, wind and rain season, and I'm held up further, due to adverse weather conditions, on the M1.

Once at Belle Vue, I finally agree to purchase a new mower for groundsman, Ken Westfield. This should keep him happy.

A stunt, planned for the home game in the FA Cup against Rushden, is for a local helicopter pilot to land on the ground with the match day ball. It promises to be quite a spectacle and one that has many potential marketing opportunities.

Don. Star's, Mike Davies, phones to say that the paper has been inundated with entries for our 'design a mascot' competition. I feel that we need a 'character' to add a little more to the pre-match entertainment. It is aimed at kids, 12 and under, and is not meant to be taken too seriously.

I leave work at 5.30 pm, travelling to Meadowhall shopping centre, near Sheffield, doing some Christmas shopping. I hate this chore.

Friday 20 November

I arrive early, in time to watch three enormous signs, paid for by The Tile Depot, Beazer Homes and Charlesworths, being erected on the front of the main stand. I never realised they would be so large, but it now clearly shows that local and national firms are backing the Club.

During the afternoon, the commercial staff and myself celebrate landing the Beazer Homes' deal, and others secured recently, by sending out for cakes.

Saturday 21 November

We have a home game against Frickley Athletic in the FA Trophy Cup. Jeremy Clarkson arrives with his film crew and we kit him out in a Rovers baseball hat, scarf and jacket. In a miserable game we lose 2-0. No Wembley for the Rovers this year.

Monday 23 November

It's foggy every day now, as I wend my way to work. An interview arranged with the *Yorkshire Post* is postponed until tomorrow. I am supposed to outline how our season is progressing. The interview was set up before the Frickley defeat.

On arrival at the ground, I receive an urgent message to call my wife at home. Her car keys are in my vehicle. I blame the children.

A post-mortem is held with Ian Snodin over Saturday's cup defeat, both of us expressing our disappointment, though agree, this season's main priority is survival.

At 2.30 pm, I meet with representatives from Gold Bond Lottery, run by Blackpool F.C. I want to pick their brains, gathering enough information to run our own lottery. I feel that a club, in a town the size of Doncaster, should be able to maintain this.

I speak to Mike Davies, who tells me there have been over 150 entries in the mascot competition. We agree to meet and choose the winner later in the week.

Great news, Beazer Homes sponsor Rovers (Photo by Paul Gilligan).

Tuesday 24 November

An earlier start than usual, as there is an 8.30 am appointment with Kevin Phelan, concerned about our current league position. We're third from bottom and in the relegation zone. Each year, three teams are relegated from Conference. I assure him that everything will be alright after Christmas.

Ian Snodin is attending a charity event later in the day, so I ask him to wear one of our new baseball jackets, to promote the Club.

At 11 am, Ian Appleyard, from the *Yorkshire Post*, interviews me. I tell him that since the take-over by Westferry there have been many improvements both on and off the field, but we still have a long way to go.

Just after 12.15 pm, Nigel Reed and myself make our way to Hallam FM radio station. I want to persuade them to give us free advertising for our home games. Disappointingly, they don't want to go down that road. There is talk of Doncaster having its own radio station. Hopefully, if that happens, we will be in a stronger position when negotiating fees with other stations.

We return to Belle Vue for a 3.45 pm meeting gathering with Kevin Phelan and Peter Smith, chairman of the Dragons Rugby Club. We go over problems arising from the Dragons playing at Belle Vue, and their involvement with the new stadium. It transpires that Westferry are not to be involved with running the rugby club.

Wednesday 25 November

My car is collected for its service, which is a nice perk.

A local milk distributor, Fieldside Dairies, has agreed to put the Club's logo on 15,000 milk bottles. This is another one of our marketing initiatives and, once again, underlines the growing credibility, currently being enjoyed with local firms.

At 1.30 pm, Phil Shaw, from the *Independent*, interviews me, for a piece centred around the positive work that has been undertaken at the Club since Westferry's take-over. I find it encouraging that the 'nationals' are interested in our progress.

By 2.30 pm, Mike Davies has arrived with two bags, full of entries, for the mascot competition. After several cups of coffee, without any biscuits – Mike Davies is not considered important enough to be offered any – we decide on a winner.

Doncaster Rovers' new mascot is … a dog, to be known as Donny Rover. The winning design was drawn by an 11-year-old girl. Whilst the whole exercise may seem an unnecessary expense, it is aimed at children 12 and under, encouraging them to watch their local football team. In time, it is hoped that the 'dog' will develop its own character and be used to promote a number of messages to children: Drink More Milk; Cross the Road Safely; Don't Go Off with Strangers; Don't Take Drugs. The design will also provide the Club with a number of merchandising opportunities.

Nigel Reed rushes in, telling me that Duncan Ferguson has been transferred from Everton to Newcastle United for £7m. We both agree this is a lot of money for someone who has suffered quite a number of injuries. No doubt, this will be the subject of many pub conversations tonight. Putting the transfer figure into a local context. The highest we have paid for a player is £15,000, and had to ask John Ryan for that.

The news of the day, in the *Don. Star*, concerns Doncaster Council Leader Malcolm Glover, who has been arrested by police for alleged irregularities in his expenses. He is just one of a number of local councillors who have been arrested – some have even been jailed – in the local government scandal dubbed 'Donnygate'.

During the evening, I watch Man. United play Barcelona. It's a fantastic game, ending in a 3-3 draw. The football on view was outstanding. I feel this could be the season where they lift the European trophy.

Thursday 26 November

During the tedious journey to work, I am kept awake by local radio station news bulletins, detailing Malcolm Glover's arrest and subsequent resignation as Council Leader.

It is usual for a football club to have team photographs taken around July or August or, at least, before the new season starts. Here, in Doncaster, we do things differently because, at 10 am, everyone poses for a late photo call. Additionally, it provides an opportunity to have a picture taken with sponsors, Beazer Homes' logo, on the players' shirts.

Later, I speak to M. McGuire at the PFA, who is unhappy that certain issues have not been resolved since the take-over.

Keith Hicks, a former colleague, now at Rochdale, 'phones me, asking for information about funding and grants. I agree to forward him some information. I'm also proud, realising that people now believe Doncaster Rovers is credible enough to offer advice on certain issues.

Doncaster Rovers, season 1998-1999.

Friday 27 November

I'm in the office by 8.00 am, clearing up any important issues, before leaving at 11 to begin a long weekend in Ireland with my wife. I dare not contemplate what she will do to me if I get home late.

Paul May arrives and I sell him a Rovers baseball jacket. He asks for staff discount, which I refuse, needing all the money we can get. Later, Paul states that a team of specialist accountants will have to be appointed as, the previous two years accounts, must be brought up-to-date. Both Westferry and Dinard have agreed to this.

A settlement has been reached over compensation with two members of the youth team staff, employed during the previous regime. They have also agreed to drop action at an Industrial Tribunal.

After failing on several occasions, I eventually manage to leave for home, not before wishing Ian Snodin good luck at tomorrow's game at Hereford.

I arrive to find that my wife has packed enough suitcases for a month's stay in the Caribbean.

Tuesday 1 December

I thoroughly enjoyed my long weekend in Ireland. After working long, ridiculous hours, it was good to have a break with my wife. I started relaxing as soon as I boarded the plane in Manchester. The passengers included Coronation Street character 'Jack Duckworth' –

everybody's idea of a down-trodden husband. Ireland is a place where I could live. And, yes, I did have a few pints of the 'black stuff'.

Unfortunately, we lost 1-0 at Hereford, and Simon Shaw was sent off. Previously, I have not been a fanatical fan or supporter of a particular football club, only I am beginning to feel a great affinity to Rovers. On hearing the result, I felt massive disappointment. The defeat means we remain third from the bottom.

Accountants Morton Thornton are at the Club all week and, hopefully, they will sort things out, as we are under pressure from Companies House to produce a set of figures. The interview that I did with the *Independent*, as part of a piece on smaller football clubs, appears today, and I am happy with it.

Nigel Reed tells me his company car is falling to pieces. After seeing him, I place, on my desk, a small marble pyramid that I bought in Ireland. It is supposed to bring good luck. I hope it does, as we need a lot of it.

We have still not received our proceeds from the cup tie at Southend, and I send a fax reminding them of the fact. I also send a copy to the FA.

Tonight we're playing Southport, at home, in the second round of the Endsleigh Trophy. The competition was started in 1980, as the Bob Lord Trophy, a national cup competition exclusively for teams in the Conference. Bob Lord was formerly chairman of Burnley F.C.

Southport put out a weak side and we win comfortably 2-0, Mark Hume scoring both goals, in front of a crowd of 949. Whilst I suppose this figure is disappointing, perhaps people are saving themselves for Saturday's FA Cup game with Rushden.

Design a Rovers mascot winner, Anna Gray, and her mother, with Mike Davies (left) and myself (Photo by Paul Gilligan).

December 1998

Wednesday 2 December

A meeting with the commercial staff and Eric Randerson (community programme officer) to plan events for Saturday's cup match. Eric has ordered 1,000 chocolate wagon wheels, from one of the companies involved in sponsoring football in the community, and we go through suggestions of how to distribute these, both inside and outside the ground.

Many people telephone requesting complimentary tickets for the game. Joan Oldale and myself work out seating arrangements for directors, sponsors, and guests.

The groundsman tells me that frost is forecast for the weekend, so we discuss ways of keeping the pitch 'playable'. It would be a nightmare if the game was called off at the last minute.

At night, I call at Dave Parker's 'mansion' in Brighouse, having further talks with him and a friend about a Rovers Internet site.

I introduce myself to the kids at 8 pm.

Thursday 3 December

I wake up early, noticing it's cold, and sensing there's frost outside. I dress quickly, and wander, in my slippers, on to the back garden, testing if the ground is frozen. This is a strange thing to do as the Rushden game is on Saturday, and it will not be played on my garden. But, in some way, I have to ease my anxiety, over the projected weather conditions.

I pack an 'overnight' bag and travel, at no more than 10 m.p.h., through the Holmfirth fog.

During the day, I hear the cost of making the Donny Rover mascot will be £3,000. I also discover there is only one match ball in stock. This situation is reminiscent of the first few days when we took control. I immediately place an order with Mitre at Huddersfield for supplies to be delivered.

Ian Green, one of the Westferry directors, has a distribution business and this includes CDs. I note that he has very kindly sent us a batch of two dozen, amongst them being various singers and bands. I pull out copies of Doris Day and Matt Munro's greatest hits. I feel sure these will evoke a reaction, if played over the PA, during a match day. Thankfully, there are more up-to-date CDs in the batch.

If we beat Rushden on Saturday, Ian and John Ryan are invited to the Third Round draw, live on television in London. They both decline the offer, and I agree to go instead.

I see a copy of a press release, written by Dave Parker, relating to a stone owl, which John Ryan is bringing along to Saturday's game. Apparently, Belle Vue's popular stand once accommodated an owl. Allegedly, when it left, the Club's fortunes plummeted. Therefore, it is hoped the stone owl will bring good fortune once again. Desperate measures, but if they work …

I work through until 7.30 pm and then check in at the Earl. Tonight, Alick Jeffrey Jnr and myself are guests of the Rovers Independent Fans Association, who are holding their Christmas party at a local social club. Needless to say, a good time is had by one and all.

Friday 4 December

Ward and Cowling come to the Club, and Paul May and myself agree the settlement figures with them. Thankfully, the whole situation ends amicably.

A little later, Paul and myself predict that tomorrow's gate receipts should be good. If this proves to be the case, it will certainly help our cash flow. Various meetings then follow with staff. Whilst I am told the pitch is frozen, frost is not forecast for tonight.

In the afternoon, there is a meeting with a rep from the World Wide Hole In One Company, and we explore various formats for games, contestants having the opportunity to win cash or a prize, these being covered by insurance. I am interested in one particular game. This is where someone is randomly picked from a football crowd and given three shots at an empty goal: one from the penalty spot, another from the edge of penalty area and a final one from the half way line.

When the rep has left, a game with a cash prize is set between Nigel Reed, Alick Jeffrey Jnr and myself. I bet the pair of them £50 they can't put the ball in the net from the half way line. So, we traipse out on to the rock hard pitch, letting the wager commence. Alick, once a Rovers apprentice, is the first to try. He runs up, miss-kicks the ball and it spirals towards the corner flag. Nigel also just misses a corner flag. I fail to score by about two yards, yet win the bet.

Rovers players celebrate a goal (Photo by Shaun Flannery).

Saturday 5 December

I leave home in bright sunshine, after inspecting the back garden and deeming it playable. For the first few miles, along the road, I am driving through thick snow. I immediately 'phone the Club on my mobile – hands free of course – asking Joan Oldale how heavily the snow has fallen in Doncaster. What snow, she asks, it's bright sunshine here, and the pitch is perfect. OK, I answer, see you later, not before telling Connor, who is with me today, to confirm we are travelling through snow.

I arrive at 10.30 am and, whilst the sun is shining, it's bitterly cold. I have a quick walk round the ground checking everything, even though I went through the same exercise yesterday. In the office, the 'phone is ringing off the hook, with people asking if the game is on. I instruct Dave Parker to put out a Press release, informing the various radio stations that the game is definitely on. Connor helps in the office, stamping tickets while I get on with some paper work.

Connor and Paul May's sons meet up again, creating much noise. The ground is filling up and the computerised turnstile figures soon whiz past 2,000. Everything is going well, the wagon wheels, being distributed to every kid in sight. Soon, the crowd is looking skywards, watching the helicopter land with the match ball. John Ryan and Max Griggs are to walk on to the pitch to collect it. One kid throws a half-eaten wagon wheel at John as he makes his way forward. I kick it off the pitch and have a word with the person responsible.

It's a beautiful day, and there is a great atmosphere swirling round the ground, the home fans are truly magnificent. The crowd figure finally reaches 5,369. The receipts

Watching the helicopter land
(Photo by Shaun Flannery).

meaning we can survive for another week. Unfortunately, the game is disappointing, ending in a 0-0 draw. We missed some good goal scoring opportunities, and it looks like our chances of winning the FA Cup hang on us beating Rushden in the re-play.

On entering the office, I find Joan, Barbara and Tracey opening a bottle of wine, celebrating a good day in the shop, with takings of around £3,000.

Monday 7 December

The topic of conversation this morning is last night's Jeremy Clarkson's Top Gear show, featuring the Club. There are differing opinions in the office about its content. Some say it was OK, others that it was too much of a mickey-take. Personally, I thought it was all right.

The match ball being delivered (Photo from Sheffield Newspapers).

John Ryan (left), helicopter pilot Tom OiMalley, and Max Griggs
(Photo from Sheffield Newspapers).

Sad news. One of our keen supporters, Ken Wilkinson, vice-chairman of Rovers Supporters Club, died after Saturday's game. He always had the Club's best interests at heart and will be sadly missed.

In the event, I don't go to London to be present at the Third Round FA Cup draw. Instead, we watch the draw on television, discovering we meet Premier League side Leeds United at home, providing, of course, we beat Rushden in the replay.

December 1998

It's a fantastic prospect and, we would, without question, ask for the tie to be switched to Elland Road, to reap the financial rewards. Naturally, our fans would be disappointed, but playing the game at Leeds could earn us in the region of £200,000, securing our short-term future.

During the course of the day, I speak to my counterpart at Rushden about our ticket allocation for the replay. We are to be given 1,200 and I tell him it's not enough. On putting the phone down, I reflect that during the previous season, nobody could have given tickets away to watch the Rovers. Now things are completely different. I discuss the ticket situation with Alick Jnr and Ian Snodin, who both agree 1,200 is insufficient. They add that the prospect of playing Leeds United has caused great excitement around the town, and a large number of fans want to encourage Rovers to victory at Rushden.

Tuesday 8 December

I speak to Rushden, who are adamant they will only allocate 1,200 tickets. I request a percentage of the ticket sales to cover our administration costs, which is refused. Unfortunately, I am not in a position to argue.

I watch the second half of a game between a Rovers XI and Bury reserves.

Later, Ian Snodin 'phones Peter Beardsley, who has become available, making him an offer to join us. Peter says he will give it careful consideration.

Wednesday 9 December

There's freezing fog and pile ups on many routes to Doncaster, so I don't reach work until mid-morning.

At 11 am, I liaise with the company designing us a cartoon character. It makes me wonder whether Chief Executive Martin Edwards, my opposite at Man. United, involves himself with similar work. Did he have a hand in designing his club's Fred the Red character? If not, I bet he wish he had done …

After consultation, I have decided to limit the Rushden replay tickets to four per person. I also agree that the staff can travel to Rushden on the coach, taking a number of our sponsors. They deserve the treat.

John Ryan says he will fund the offer to Peter Beardsley. Ian Snodin will contact the player tonight.

At the end of the day, there is a dilemma deciding which route to take home. I wish I was staying overnight in Doncaster. The journey takes two and a half hours.

Thursday 10 December

The Rushden tickets are available today from 10 am and, when I arrive at 9 am, there's already a long queue eagerly waiting to purchase them. Sales will be conducted from the Club shop, which is a deliberate ploy on my part, encouraging people to buy items while they are on the premises.

Alick Jeffrey Jnr predicts we will sell out by the end of the day. We have a small wager over this prospect.

I converse with the local police about playing the Leeds United game at Belle Vue. They say it will have to be switched to Leeds. I let them know that I am unhappy with this decision. If we didn't need the money so desperately, we would definitely want to hold the game in Doncaster.

Ian tells me that Peter Beardsley has declined our offer, saying he has received a fantastic proposal from another club. I discuss this with John Ryan and, whilst having him here would have been an exciting prospect, we are not too disappointed.

At 8 pm, 1,027 tickets have been sold. A dejected Alick Jeffrey Jnr claims that I have deliberately held back tickets to win the wager. I must be slipping, because I had not even thought of that trick. I also wonder when the Club last sold this amount of tickets in a day. During a late conversation with Paul May, he states Rovers are now attracting the town's attention for all the right reasons.

Friday 11 December

The remaining Rushden tickets go within the first half hour of the shop opening. Many fans are disappointed at being unable to buy any. Some say they will try and obtain tickets at Rushden on the match day. I have to tell them that none will be sold to Rovers fans.

Today is the funeral of Ken Wilkinson, and we send condolences and a Club representative.

I stay over night at the Earl, enabling me to be on the team coach, bound for Welling, at 8 am tomorrow.

Saturday 12 December

Welling is a club I'd never even heard of before this season – no disrespect intended. I notice that John Ryan's Bentley is already at the ground and, when I join him in the Board Room, he introduces me to his guest, Peter Wetzel, a former Rovers director.

The ground is small, though one of the Welling directors tells me they have plans for a new development. There's a meagre crowd of 761 and I'm expecting the game to be a tough one for us, as the squad is missing Shaw, Ybarra and Kirkwood.

After a positive first half performance, we are winning 1-0, through a Mark Hume goal. Unfortunately, we don't play as well during the second period, Steve Nicol receives a rib injury and they equalize. We, somehow, hang on to the 1-1 score line until the end of the match.

Monday 14 December

The BBC interview me about the Rushden replay. Of late, I seem to have been in touch with the media a lot.

Rushden are still causing problems for me, saying they will only issue eight car park tickets for our directors. Despite my protests they won't budge on the issue.

All our office staff seem to be going to the match, so we decide to close the office for the afternoon.

December 1998

During the evening, we stage a fund-raising event at Doncaster's Karisma night club, where the Gutter Band – a 70s glam rock outfit-perform for us. The attendance is poor, Rovers supporters probably saving their energies for tomorrow's game.

Tuesday 15 December

It goes without saying, we have a big day ahead, the ultimate prize being a third round clash with Leeds United.

During the early part of the morning, people are still phoning, in the hope of getting tickets. I estimate that around 300-400 will travel to Rushden without any. As Ian and Glynn Snodin climb on to the team coach, I wish them good luck. I'm travelling separately, due to an afternoon appointment with Paul May at his offices in Northampton. On completing our business, Paul and two guests accompany me to Rushden. There's traffic congestion along the approach roads, indicating there'll be a sizeable crowd. Rushden's ground can hold around 6,000, and from a distance looks quite impressive. However, officials appear to have forgotten to erect any car park signs. Ironically, on finding the car park, and announcing we are Doncaster Rovers' directors, we are not asked for our passes.

Following a short spell in the Board Room, talking to Chairman Max Griggs and his directors, we watch Rovers warming up on the pitch. Whilst Ian played in the first game, he has left himself out of this one, carrying a slight injury. Personally, I'm disappointed that he's side-lined.

Back in the Board Room, there's quite a turn out of Doncaster officials and friends, including Ian Green, Kevin Phelan, Mike Collet and Paul May. With only minutes to kick off, a digital turnstile counter on view, clicks past 5,000. I guess there's more than 1,200 Doncaster fans in the ground, and they are out-singing and chanting the Rushden supporters, even during the warm up period.

I know Rushden are a good side and are tipped to win the league, though on a good day I feel we are a match for anyone. Yet, four minutes into the game, Mark Hume makes an awful challenge and is sent off. When this happens, I feel it is not going to be our day, especially when a Rushden player takes an obvious dive, and they are awarded a penalty, quickly making the score 1-0.

In time, we manage to draw level from a Colin Sutherland goal, though Rushden press home their superiority, and win 4-2. Rovers' efforts were outstanding, only matched by our fans, singing at the tops of their voices from the first minute until the last. I don't think I have ever felt as proud as I did after the game. Our directors and officials are pleased with the team's performance. The Mark Hume sending off, early on in the game, definitely sealed our fate, not being able to cope with their extra man. Sadly, we have missed the opportunity of reaping the financial rewards of meeting Leeds in the next round. However, we are still in contention with the Endsleigh Trophy. And, who knows, we could win that.

After only fourth months of Westferry being in charge, Kevin Phelan says he is pleased at the way things appear to have been turned round on the field. He hands out £100 for the players to have a drink on him. I think this is a nice gesture. The atmosphere in the dressing room

Donny Rover relaxes (Photo from Sheffield Newspapers).

is one of extreme disappointment. Ian and Glynn say the players could not give any more, agreeing the sending off cost us the game. Hopefully Mark will learn from the mistake, being his second sending off this season.

I set off along the M1, bound for Doncaster, staying there over tonight. I pass several coaches carrying our fans home, and feel proud to be associated with them. They are truly remarkable and, with their backing, Doncaster Rovers can go far.

Wednesday 16 December

Many calls are received, congratulating us on the performance at Rushden.

A number of newspapers concentrate on the impending Rushden/Leeds cup fixture, Rushden insisting they will play the game at home, not switching it to Leeds.

It's back to reality in the office, and I meander through the day, debating with Ian Snodin, Saturday's home game with Dover, and staffing over Christmas.

Those on the coach, carrying the sponsors to yesterday's game, had a good time, Alick Jnr, Nigel and other staff members taking most of the day to recover. It appears that card schools and Karaoke were the order of the day.

An early finish, at around 5 pm, wanting to get home to the kids, as I've not seen them for two days.

Thursday 17 December

A dull day, with no executive decisions being made. I arrive home at 6.50 pm and Connor greets me, saying: 'Dad, what are you doing home early?'

I just give him a hug, hoping he understands why I am away so often.

December 1998

Friday 18 December

Our groundsman, Ken Westfield, hobbles into the office, after undergoing a knee replacement operation, and he appears to be recovering quite well. It reminds me that I need one too. But, at 34, I'll wait a little longer, before having it done on the NHS, otherwise I'll be paying out to have further replacements, thereafter, at 10-year intervals.

A fax is received, illustrating the projected Donny Rover design. It's very good.

I receive copies of the programme for tomorrow's Dover game. To my horror, I discover something mentioned in an article about the previous regime, that I insisted on being omitted, has been printed. I am not impressed and attempts to locate the programme's editor, to express my annoyance, prove fruitless. For the remainder of the afternoon, several staff members and myself, tear out the offending page from each programme, with a competition being staged for the 'neatest tearer'.

Saturday 19 December

Considering there's less than a week to go before Christmas, I'm pleased with the crowd for this afternoon's game, numbering 2,119.

I find the programme editor and give him an almighty bollocking. A little later, I am approached by the writer of the offending article, and her father, who is a solicitor. He tells me the piece was OK. Unfortunately, I disagree with them. We are trying to move forward not get bogged down in the past.

Twenty minutes into the game and we're 3-0 down, developing into one of the most eventful contests I have ever seen. Eventually, we claw back to 3-3, only to trail 4-3, minutes later. At the final whistle, we win 5-4, the crowd going berserk.

John Ryan wastes no time, after the game, shooting back to Manchester, where his company, Transform, is holding its Christmas party. As several members of Rovers' staff, including myself, are invited I follow shortly afterwards. Just when I believe the journey is going well, I encounter black ice on the Holmfirth to Saddleworth road, the car skidding out of control, before colliding, at speed, with a dry-stone wall. I went through all the procedures to avoid the skid, but to no avail, the car now balancing precipitously over a 10 ft drop. After remaining motionless, for what seems to be an eternity, I scramble to safety, out of the passenger side, being unable to open the door on my side. Fortunately, someone comes to my assistance, and a passing police car stops to check if I'm OK. It was a terrifying experience and I'm badly shaken, but have no major injuries, just a bump on the head. I 'phone my wife, telling her about the incident, and John Ryan, saying I may be a little late in joining the party. The police arrange for the car to be towed away, and kindly give me a lift home. I put on a brave face, trying to be macho, eventually arriving, only half-an-hour late, at the hotel, to meet Ian Snodin, John Bowden and Alick Jeffrey Jnr. We climb into a taxi, making for Manchester City's ground, where the function is being held, passing through the largest wrought-iron security gates I have ever seen.

Monday 21 December

I stayed in bed most of Sunday, suffering the effects of the crash. At the time, I did not believe it was too bad, but now I keep thinking I could have been killed. Today, this is preying on my mind.

Not having a vehicle and still sore from the crash, I catch a train from Stockport, arriving in Doncaster early in the afternoon, becoming a blur.

After my ordeal, it seemed a good idea to still attend the party. Now, I'm not so sure. But, I hate letting people down. Everybody was in the Christmas spirit, then the spirit got into everybody.

I feel worse as the day progresses, and stay overnight at the Earl.

Tuesday 22 December

Paul May arrives and we finalise a number of financial matters before the Christmas break, making sure the electricity is not cut off ...

At some point during the day, I'm taken to Charlesworths, where my car has been delivered, to await repairs. I refuse a vehicle that's offered to me, in the mean time, on the grounds that it is too small for my bulky frame, finally settling for a Ford Focus.

Still replaying Saturday's trauma through my mind, I drive home gingerly, pausing at the crash scene, and examining the damage to the wall. Finally, I realise how lucky I am to emerge unscathed.

Wednesday 23 December

Club Secretary, Joan Oldale, is not at work today, beginning her Christmas holidays early this year. Everyone else in the office is winding down and we all have a relatively quiet day, making sure everything is in place for the holiday fixtures. In contrast, Tracey has an extremely busy time in the shop. I offer to buy her a bottle of champagne if sales, over the Christmas period, reach £35,000.

I work late, partly because the shop is open until 9.00 pm, feeling I should be around in case any problems arise.

Thursday 24 December

I arrive early, noticing the office staff have a spring in their step, probably anticipating being allowed to leave before 5 pm. I insist everybody stays until that time, yet know I will let them go after lunch. A. Jeffrey Jnr and myself pop round to the large Asda store nearby, having a word with the manager Peter Brigden. We buy some of the best wine to hand out to the staff later on. I also obtain a bottle of Moet, as I expect Tracey to surpass the sales target she has been set. She deserves the champagne for effort alone.

I allow the staff to open a bottle of wine, and have a drink, as long as it's out of public view. At 1.30 pm I let them go home, after being reliably informed that's what they were about to do anyway. I stand under the mistletoe though nobody takes the hint, except A. Jeffrey Jnr, fooling around as usual.

I drive home, thinking about our shop takings over the last six weeks. They're more than those achieved over the previous three years.

In the house, my wife is wrapping more presents.

December 1998/January 1999

Saturday, Boxing Day, 26 December

Today, we're entertaining Leek Town at home, and Elise and the boys are with me. I'm, obligingly, wearing new socks and tie, Elise is resplendent in a new outfit, while the kids are playing with some of their toys. I muse on how many other dads in the crowd will be wearing Christmas presents.

As we drive over the tops, there's no let up in the weather, a howling wind and driving rain lashing the car. Normally, Boxing Day football matches are well attended, only I feel the weather conditions may deter some folk from turning out. It's usual too, over the Christmas period, for teams to play a local Derby game. Not so this year for us, as we play Hednesford away on 28 December, and Leek away on 2nd January.

The crowd reaches 3,520, and there's a good atmosphere at the start of the game. Disappointingly, we lose 1-0, our league position still remaining perilous. On the positive side, over £2,000 has been taken in the shop.

After the game, in the Board Room, there is a sombre un-festive mood. Yet, we have a chance to turn our fortunes around with a match in two days time.

Monday 28 December

I travel alone to Hednesford Town, finding those associated with the club to be hospitable. We take the lead through a Mark Hume goal, only to see it cancelled out by one, blatantly offside. This spoils what, otherwise, would have been a thoroughly deserved win for us.

I travel back up the M6, to play a game with Connor on his new Sony Play Station.

Saturday 2 January 1999

Today we're away at Leek Town, their ground being only about an hour's drive from where I live. The topic of conversation, when I'm in the Board Room, is a £50,000 offer for one of their players, Hugh McCauley. Whilst he seemed impressive last season, I wouldn't pay that amount for him. He will be sold, I'm sure, as Leek are eager to bolster their dwindling finances.

Over 600 Doncaster fans are in the crowd, numbering 1,365. It's a lively game, ending in another 1-1, which is not good for us, as we slip to 21st in the table. With two points from nine, over the Christmas period, we'll have to turn things around soon.

The gulf between the foreign leagues and the Conference is brought into sharp focus with the news of Steve McManaman being offered £110,000 a week to sign for Real Madrid. Gianluca Viali says he will match this if McManaman signs for Chelsea. I wonder if he will be paid in Euros or Pesetas, if deciding on a move to Spain, the Euro being launched this week. People say it is obscene that a footballer is paid this amount. They are only worth that amount if someone is willing to pay it.

Over Christmas we resign Kevin McIntyre on loan from Tranmere.

FOOTBALL CONFERENCE
(upto & including Jan 2, 1999)

	P	W	D	L	F	A	Ps
Kettering T.	26	15	6	5	36	18	51
Cheltenham T.	23	14	7	2	43	17	49
Rushden & D.	20	11	6	3	38	16	39
Stevenage Boro'	22	9	9	4	28	22	36
Yeovil Town	21	9	8	4	35	25	35
Kingstonian	22	9	8	5	31	30	35
Morecambe	24	10	5	9	44	45	35
Hednesford T.	22	8	9	5	28	25	33
Hereford Utd.	24	9	5	10	28	28	32
Hayes	21	10	2	9	25	29	32
Kidderminster H.	22	9	4	9	33	25	31
Northwich Vic.	24	8	7	9	26	28	31
Dover Ath.	22	7	8	7	29	26	29
Woking	22	8	5	9	25	26	29
Leek Town	23	7	5	11	33	33	26
Southport	21	5	9	7	26	31	24
Barrow	24	6	6	12	25	39	24
Forest Green R.	21	5	7	9	25	30	22
Welling Utd.	24	4	9	11	23	38	21
Telford Utd.	23	4	9	10	23	40	21
ROVERS	**23**	**4**	**7**	**12**	**24**	**34**	**19**
Farnborough T.	22	4	5	13	24	47	17

Conference table, showing Rovers are steadily improving.

Monday 4 January

All the office staff, the players and myself, return to work. It's the first time, in a while, that I've had a Christmas break. I now look forward to the summer holidays, already booked by my wife. I am also invited on an 'end-of-the-season' trip to Spain – if we stay up – that John Ryan has organised for the players, management and some of the staff.

I discuss with Ian Snodin, the team's performances in the Christmas games. He mentions that his search for new players is still ongoing, attempting to guarantee us safety from the drop. Any new players will still have to be funded by John Ryan, even though he will not take-over for a number of months. A true Rovers fan!

Tuesday 5 January

Former Rovers supremo Ken Richardson appears at Sheffield Crown Court, facing charges in relation to the 1995 Belle Vue main stand fire. Groundsman Peter White and Club Secretary Joan Oldale are also to be there, but not as key as witnesses. They will have to attend court each day until they are called.

Dave Bassett has been sacked as manager of Nottingham Forest.

John Ryan has agreed he will fund the purchase of Kevin McIntyre from Tranmere. We also take defender Stuart Rimmer on loan from Man. City.

Wednesday 6 January

In the evening, Alick Jeffrey Jnr and myself, watch Barnsley Reserves play Man. City Reserves. It's all hands to the pumps in the hope of spotting new players. This helps Ian and Glynn who, on average, watch 10 games each week, travelling many miles. Sometimes they watch several games each day. At half time, Alick and myself discuss the quality of pies available. Later, we note there are many quality players on view though, it is unlikely they would be affordable to us.

'Torch Belle Vue for ten grand'

What Rovers' ex-boss is alleged to have offered the former SAS soldier

Thursday 7 January

Paul May arrives with an accountant, to bring things up-to-date, as John Ryan is having Due Diligence done on the Club. This is basically a full assessment of our income, expenditure and debts. It is also an indication that something tangible is now happening, with regard to the take-over.

A newspaper article reveals that Notts. County are demanding £2m. for a 15-year-old player, Jermaine Pennant. It will be interesting to see if they receive any bids.

Friday 8 January

I talk with P. Smith, at Doncaster Dragons, about the new stadium, and how they might share the facilities with ourselves.

Bury F.C. have made an approach for one of our junior players. I speak to Ian Snodin, who will not oppose the move, the player not figuring in his long-term plans.

Everyone seems to be chasing us to pay debts, and these are difficult to meet, given the cash flow problems. And, we're one down in the commercial dept., Alick Jeffrey Jnr away in Tenerife for a week.

In an interesting move, Ron Atkinson has become Nottingham Forest's manager. I have a lot of respect for him, though believe their problems this season are insurmountable.

A FORMER SAS soldier set fire to Doncaster Rovers' ground after the club's ex-boss offered £10,0000, a court heard.

Ex-Doncaster Rovers supremo Ken Richardson ordered Alan Kristiansen to torch the club's stand in the hope Rovers could build a new stadium, Sheffield Crown Court was told.

Giving evidence at Richardson's trial for conspiracy to commit

BY DAVID KESSEN

arson, Kristansen recalled how he drove to Belle Vue with three others and used petrol and diesel to torch the club's main stand.

He was to be paid £10,000 for the job but never received the cash, he claimed.

Richardson, an Isle of Man-based businessman who quit the club last year, denies the charge.

Kristiansen told the jury he had phoned Richardson to confirm the job and was told "I've had nothing but bad press" – a code signalling Kristiansen to go ahead.

Former SAS man Kristiansen, of Hexham, Northumbria, said 61-year-old Richardson had asked him to burn down the stand after meeting him at Belle Vue.

Kristiansen is currently awaiting sentence after admitting causing the fire in June 1995.

Roger Keen QC, prosecuting, asked Kristiansen about the meeting at Belle Vue and was told: "He was telling me how they were the worst club in the league and that the council wouldn't give them any money to improve the ground.

"We walked round and he suggested to me that a man of my

experience with fire damage could help the club, as he had plans to build a new football stadium on the ground.

Kristiansen said Richardson told him the fire damage would enable the club to take down the stands and build a new stadium.

But he left a mobile phone at the scene of the crime – and police traced it back to him and arrested him in the North East.

He also used a traceable credit card to buy petrol for the fire while being recorded on security cameras.

The trial continues.

Headline from the Doncaster Star, 15 January 1999

Saturday 9 January

I'm excited about today's home game with Cheltenham Town, arguably the best team in the Conference and, I'm sure, at the end of the season, they will be crowned champions. It will be interesting to see how we play against them

Before the kick-off, I converse with John Ryan and Paul May, expressing concern about our league position. They say it is crucial that we start winning games to avoid slipping out of the Conference.

At 2.50 pm, a presentation is made to Eric Randerson, who has spent 10 years with the Club as community programme officer. This is thoroughly deserved, working under very difficult circumstances.

The Board Room is very quiet at half time as we're trailing 2-0. Earlier in the game, a former Rovers player, Neil Grayson, gave a two-fingered salute to the crowd, emphasising the score line. Consequently, they jeered him, every time he touched the ball. It was a very foolish gesture and the game does not need this type of behaviour.

In the second period, we fight back to gain a creditable draw, with goals by Duerden and Goodwin, who was outstanding. Kevin McIntyre added an extra dimension to our defence, and young Rimmer played well too. Unfortunately, there is some crowd trouble and more police are called, though this proves to be unnecessary, with everyone calming down.

In the Board Room everyone is pleased that we've managed to take a point from a team of Cheltenham's calibre. But, we discover that other teams – Farnborough and Telford – fighting for survival at the foot of the Conference, like ourselves, have won their games. Therefore, everyone is still as concerned about our league position, as they were two hours earlier.

The crowd of 3,082 turns out to be the highest Conference gate of the day. I'm also delighted that over £1,200 has been taken in the shop, Tracey telling me we need more stock.

Monday 11 January

With secretary Joan Oldale away at the Richardson trial, we are short staffed.

I make arrangements for our stadium manager, Albert Paget, and myself to meet the police's match day commander. We're being charged for the their attendance at our home matches which I believe is unfair, so we'll try to do something about it.

In the evening, I watch Man. Utd with John Ryan.

Tuesday 12 January

Before getting up, I peer, blearily, through the bedroom window, after hearing snow is causing problems in certain areas. Whilst there's none outside in the garden, I leave early, fearing the worst. On approaching Holmfirth, snow is several feet deep. I drive with extra care, memories of the accident flooding into my mind. At Holmfirth, I have to retrace my steps, trying several different routes, which are all blocked. It's a nightmare situation, and eventually arrive at work three-and-a-half hours late. Once again I consider moving to Doncaster or staying over night more often.

January 1999

I see Paul May, and he is unhappy with one or two issues and I have to take the blame. It goes to show that we have come a long way, but still a considerable distance from where we want to be.

I set off for home around 9 pm, discovering the snow has completely disappeared.

Wednesday 13 January

Following yesterday's talk with Paul May, I hold a staff meeting, to re-focus everyone, making sure that all our systems are in place, and that everyone has signed the confidentiality clause in their contracts.

At Saturday's home game, we are launching our penny-a-ticket scheme for kids. It's another marketing ploy and we're hoping to sell/give away around 4,000 tickets. I predict only 25%-30% of ticket holders will actually attend.

P. May and Kevin Phelan confer with John Ryan, and it now looks as if John will be joined by a partner, Peter Wetzel, in the take-over deal. Until that happens, it's just business as usual for the rest of us.

Ian Snodin tells me that his wife is three-and-a-half months pregnant, with their fifth child. And, to think that I believed he spent most of his evenings on scouting trips …

I leave at 7.30 pm, reluctantly listening to the Leeds/Rushden replay on the car radio. The first game at Rushden ended in a draw. I ponder on what might have been for us, if we had beaten them. So, I hope that Rushden are 'stuffed'. But then, the rational person in me intervenes and reflects that, despite what people may think, there are quality teams in the Conference, Rushden being one of them. If they can beat Leeds, it will give the Conference added credibility.

Thursday 14 January

Leeds have beaten Rushden 3-1, but there are the usual cup upsets: Swansea were 1-0 winners over West Ham, and Fulham put out Southampton by the same score.

Clinton is facing impeachment because of his perjury. Many young people have learned a new word with impeachment, though older ones will remember it was instrumental in ousting President Nixon. I can't help but wonder how a person like Clinton, so much in the public eye, thought he could get away with having a relationship, sexual or otherwise, 'with that woman'.

Friday 15 January

At 11 am, Albert Paget and myself parley with the police. We hammer out a match day policing policy, and a 'statement of intent' is agreed by both parties.

The penny-a-ticket scheme is going well though, for the remainder of the day, I avoid phone calls from kit manufacturers Asics, chasing us for money. We just donít have it.

John Ryan has agreed a deal with Tranmere over Kevin McIntyre – £5,000 down now, and another £5,000 later, if we stay in the Conference.

There's excitement when sweet manufacturers Bassetts provide us with 1000 cola-flavour Whoppa bars, to be given away free at tomorrow's game. We all sample them, reminding us of our school days.

I am informed that John Ryan's 'Due Diligence' has been completed.

Ken Scott, whose company handles PR for the Conference, 'phones and I tell him about our latest promotional ploy for kids. He thinks this is brilliant and I agree to inform him regularly about the schemes we are employing.

At the end of the day, I learn the weather forecast is bleak for Saturday, and I'm worried this may determine how many 'penny-a-ticket' kids turn up.

Saturday 16 January

Today it's Morecambe at home.

Ian tells me he has looked at a player currently with Chester, a club badly in need of finance, though decides he is not suitable for us, although some others could be useful.

The ground is seemingly full of kids with their parents. I can sense they feel excitement, some attending a football match for the first time. I glance into the shop, noticing that kids are buying anything with a Rovers logo on it.

A crowd of 4,251 generates a great atmosphere. Shortly before the kick off, news of the Kevin McIntyre deal is announced and he is paraded before the crowd. Unfortunately, that is the only excitement during the first half, ending with us 1-0 down, and there are a few boos, mouthed in frustration, as the players traipse off the field.

Nevertheless, in an outstanding second half performance, where Dave Penney scores two cracking goals, Rovers romp home as winners. We have played four games in 1999 and have yet to be beaten. Is the tide now turning?

Joan informs me that 701 kids attended the game.

Monday 18 January

John Ryan, Peter Wetzel and Kevin Phelan arrive, to talk to the office and playing staff about the take-over. It will be interesting to see what happens. I wonder how I will fit in? The two men confirm that the take-over is going to happen, though they are unable to give an exact completion date, predicting it may be April or May. They talk about where we are now as a Club and where we want to go. John Ryan is someone who I feel is trustworthy and he says he wants continuity. In short, the new company is not looking to replace me or anyone else. The new stadium is discussed and the whole event passes off in a light-hearted way. Everyone seemed quite happy afterwards. However, once the take-over has occurred, things may be different. Paul May's future role is uncertain. I hope he stays as we have worked well together, mainly trying to make ends meet.

January 1999

Tuesday 19 January

Yorkshire Television interview Laurie Sheffield, a former Rovers centre forward, and myself, about various matters, including the present situation at the Club and the Richardson trial.

Wednesday 20 January

Today John Ryan, Paul May and yours truly have an appointment with the FA. I leave home at 6.30 am, travelling first to Paul May's offices, and encounter the usual traffic jams along the way.

We drive to the outskirts of London, parking Paul's car at a friends', continuing the remainder of the journey by Tube. The FA's meetings are still being held at the Merchant Navy Hotel, and John eventually joins us there.

Peter Wetzel (Photo by Shaun Flannery).

We plan our tactics, the purpose of the visit being to give details of the new take-over. When the meeting eventually begins, we introduce ourselves, but are curtly told, only those who will speak should make an introduction. The FA then proceed to ask far-reaching questions about Dinard, the identity of Westferry and other personal matters. Paul May politely tells them certain issues are none of their business. We leave without anything being concluded or decided.

Outside, we bump into two representatives from Barrow F.C. They have been summoned to the FA about alleged problems at the club. Financially, they are at death's door, and desperately looking at ways and means to give the club the kiss of life. We are interested in one of their players, Neil Morton so, after John calls Ian Snodin, confirming this, an offer is made there and then, in the street. It is quickly accepted, subject to the player agreeing personal terms and training with us for a few days to make sure he is fit.

My wife is fascinated by Feng Shui, aromatherapy and other weird and wonderful beliefs and customs. Small Buddhas are dotted round the house, and there's a picture of mountains behind my desk at work, supposedly to give me strength and support. When I arrive home, at 8 pm, she's prepared an eye pack for me and there are other strange potions in the fridge. Lighted candles flicker everywhere and a diffuser emits strange aromas. After having a gruelling day, travelling to and from London, a smile creases my face, anticipating a romantic evening, until she says all this is to help me have a good night's sleep.

Thursday 21 January

The Rovers logo incorporates a Viking helmet so, as another promotional ploy, we have ordered a number of replica helmets, to be handed out to kids at the next home game. They are delivered today and, hopefully, they will prove to be a success.

Good news. The Nationwide Building Society, already sponsoring the national side, and several leagues, have agreed to support the Conference, giving it a much needed credibility boost. Maybe now, pressure can be brought to bear, supporting the argument for three teams to be promoted back into the Football League, instead of one.

On the way home, I collide head-on with another vehicle, both of us travelling at great speed. The other driver thought he could easily overtake someone on a winding road, unable to see me approaching from the other direction. If I'd been in the small vehicle, originally offered by Charlesworths, before accepting the Ford Focus, I would have been in real trouble. My car's in a ditch and there's glass everywhere. Fortunately, whilst I'm badly shaken, and bruised, nothing is broken.

The other driver is all right too, only suffering whiplash injuries. Having witnessed the incident, several people have stopped and are hurling abuse at him. He apologises to me, saying he was in a hurry. If I wasn't in such pain, I would punch his lights out.

I search for my mobile, trying to think of how to tell my wife I've been in another car crash. In the meantime, I consider resigning from my job as Chief Executive to take up a new role as a crash test dummy. I'm in a daze when I speak to Elise, and the pungent smell of the inflated airbag is still lingering in the air.

The police arrive and take statements. The other driver and myself are breathalysed but everything is OK. I'm driven to Oldham hospital by a policeman, a girl on the reception saying she was in one of my classes at school. Every time I've been to a hospital there's invariably the same clientele in the waiting room: an Asian family chattering away in Urdu, a drunk singing and trying to engage everyone in conversation, an English family shouting at a kid, and workers with a weird and wonderful array of injuries.

Several X-Rays are taken and prove I have nothing broken, though one doctor is concerned about the whiplash I have suffered, requesting my return in a few days time. I arrive home at around midnight, my wife showing concern, and suggesting that I ought to stay overnight more often in Doncaster. I'm in that much pain I agree to anything.

Friday 22 January

I stay at home, spending most of the day in bed. I talk briefly with Paul May and John Ryan. Paul May sounds off about the number of crap drivers on the roads these days.

I keep re-living the crash and feel nervous about sitting behind a wheel again. I am bloody sick of all the accidents, fog and traffic chaos …

Saturday 23 January

Still feeling unwell, I'm staying at home, missing our away game at Rushden. Ian Snodin is another absentee as, today, is the only opportunity for seeing a player in Scotland.

January 1999

During the afternoon, I fall asleep, waking up around 5.10 pm, quickly searching through the teletext for the Rovers result. I discover they have won 3-1, Duerden scoring a hat-trick, with an own goal by Steve Nicol thrown in for good measure. I leap for joy, before realising how much pain I'm in. Eventually, I speak to Glynn, who's obviously delighted with the result. He also mentions that around 1,000 Rovers fans travelled to the game.

That's just my luck, missing the one game I wanted to see.

Monday 25 January

I'm still off work, but learn that Barrow F.C. have been in court with a winding up order. This is bad news for us because if they fold, the points we have taken from them, will be subtracted from our total, keeping us firmly in the relegation zone.

I speak to Paul May about the Rushden game, which he attended, their ground being reasonably close to his offices. He enthuses about the way the team performed and the amount of support they received. I think he's now become quite a fan himself.

Wednesday 27 January

I have a 9.15 am appointment at the hospital for a check up. They reluctantly say I'm fit enough to return to work. I suspect most 'normal' people, after suffering a similar ordeal, would have been absent for months.

Ken Richardson is found guilty, but will be sentenced at a later date. Hopefully, this will now put behind us the legacy of the previous regime. Whilst I know the fans will never forget what was, arguably, the most traumatic time in the Club's history, we must go forward.

Thursday 28 January

The morning journey is by train. I still feel very sore but, being the boss, I cannot really afford to have any time off work – another one of management's perks.

A number of people 'phone, asking if we have heard about Ken Richardson's conviction.

We are informed by the local Council that urgent safety work needs to be carried out before the next home game. For some reason, new problems have been highlighted. It appears they have been there for several years without being noticed. But, the fans' safety is paramount, and will never be compromised.

The evening is spent in Doncaster.

Friday 29 January

I tell Ian Snodin that I will travel on the team coach tomorrow.

I pick up a video of the Rovers v. Rushden game, which I missed last Saturday, before collecting another courtesy car, driving home slowly through fog and rain. Reflecting once more on the most recent accident, I can honestly say I have never been as frightened. I only hope the mental traumas, I suffered, will disappear as quickly as my aches and pains.

I drive slowly over the tops, on what seems to be the longest journey of my life. I suppose the only way to conquer a fear is to meet it head on. We shall see.

Saturday 30 January

Kettering, who we meet today, are top of the Conference. I feel the game will be a good test of how far we have progressed. Again, we are well supported, with over 1,000 Rovers fans in the ground. Seeing them in numbers, at away games, gives the players an added boost. It is also worth noting that we appear to be taking more fans to away fixtures than attended games at home last season.

To everyone's delight, we emerge victorious, thanks to an 88th minute goal from Ian Duerden, his fifth this month. We are now unbeaten in six games, winning three on the trot, and only losing two out of the last twelve. This kind of form could save us from the drop and, who knows, see us win the Endsleigh Cup. What a fitting end to the season, that would be.

Monday 1 February

Rumours abound that a former Rovers player, Graeme Jones, is on his way from Wigan Athletic to Hull City, in a £200,000 deal. If these are true, there will be a windfall for us, because of a sell-on clause in his contract.

The newspaper headlines are largely concerned with the comments England Coach Glenn Hoddle has made about disabled people. If these are true, he should be sacked without question. Personally, I never fail to be amazed at the number of 'clangers' dropped by people in the public spotlight. Hoddle is one of my all time greats but, sadly, the intelligence footballers display on the field is not always mirrored off it.

Rovers player, Colin Sutherland, has accumulated 10 bookings. One more and he will be fined. Whilst some of these cautions were justified, I feel that the FA's disciplinary procedures need overhauling. The way football was played in the days of Hunter, Bremner, Charlton, Stiles, R. Harris, and MacKay is long gone. If teams had those players today they would be travelling to the FA's offices so often, they might even consider building a hotel nearby. Whilst some of the FA's new rules are OK, many well-disciplined players are also picking up bookings, unnecessarily.

Ian Duerden trying to keep his shirt on (Photo by Shaun Flannery).

Tuesday 2nd February

My youngest son, Nolan, was awake all night, suffering from a virus. Consequently, I'm very tired this morning, not looking forward to the journey ahead.

Ian Duerden has won the Conference's award for the goal scorer of the month. The team has won the League's award for the performance of the month, with the 3-1 win over Rushden. A sure sign that events are now following a positive course.

February 1999

Glynn is travelling to Scotland, trying to organise a scouting network up there. At the present time, Ian and Glynn are spending too much time, scouting themselves. So, we aim to put systems into place that will ease the work-load on them.

We've decided to the make the home game against Yeovil on 13 February, Viking Day. This is one of John Ryan's ideas.

People should not take these schemes too seriously. We are only trying to create themes and develop our own branding. With the Viking helmets, we are just 'dipping our toes in the water'.

The FA is to make an announcement about Hoddle's future. I doubt they would be commenting if he was staying in the job.

Wednesday 3 February

The repairs being carried out on my vehicle, the one involved in the crash on the night of the Transform Christmas party, will be completed by the end of the week.

I receive a letter from the police, confirming we will be allowed 'police-free' matches. Thank goodness for that! Other mail includes a report, titled 'The World's Richest Clubs', written by accountants Deloitte & Touche. I debate whether to glance at it or not, knowing Doncaster Rovers will not be mentioned.

Manchester United are the richest club (with an £89,939,000 turn over), no surprises there, a gap of £30m dividing them and second placed Barcelona, and £60m separating them from Arsenal in 20th position. The reason for United being £30m ahead of anyone else is largely through the success of their merchandising operation, and their branding being known throughout the world. However, I feel that the Spanish and Italian clubs will come to the fore in a few years time. They will study United's success and emulate it.

Hoddle goes. Did he resign or was he sacked, is the question many people are asking.

Thursday 4 February

There is another sportsman's dinner tonight, and I check with the commercial boys that everything is organised.

We do not have another home game for 10 days so the cash flow is tight.

The papers are speculating on who will be the new England manager, with Doncaster's favourite footballing son, Kevin Keegan, topping everyone's list.

Ian Wright announces he is retiring from international matches. In my opinion, he was never good enough to play for his country. Whilst he was an outstanding Arsenal player, some players cannot reproduce their club success at international level. But, football is all about opinions. That is why it is such a great sport.

During the evening's dinner I meet writer (and editor of this book), Peter Tuffrey, who says it would be a good idea to put all the notes I have scribbled, about Rovers this season, into some order and publish them in a book.

But, I'm unsure now, Ed.

Friday 5 February

A quiet day, after last night's successful sportsman's dinner.

I collect my vehicle, now repaired, and pause on the way home, showing it the damage inflicted on the dry-stone wall.

We have no game tomorrow, and I wonder what to do. The Five Nations Rugby Union matches are on television so, no doubt, they will provide some entertainment …

Monday 8 February

A private firm of structural engineers has arrived to carry out a survey on the popular stand, as a Council officer has raised a question about its safety. Stadium manager Albert Paget, and myself spend all morning with them.

During the afternoon, a conversation is held with the Club solicitor over our licensing applications and a plan to convert a porta-cabin into a bar.

John Ryan has arranged for Stuart Hall – of It's A Knockout fame – to do a voice-over on a radio advert, promoting Saturday's fixture. Previous radio ads have been successful, increasing match day attendances.

I once read a survey on football grounds, which stated that many were rarely, if ever, filled to capacity. A ground, which held 10,000, only ever managed to attract figures of 2,000-3,000. Clearly, clubs should encourage higher attendances through marketing techniques.

Tuesday 9 February

There is a crisis. A Council officer, having consulted with the structural engineers, says that urgent safety work has to be carried out to the popular stand before Saturday's game. If it can't be done, we will have to close that section. Carrying out the work will further exacerbate our cash flow. Surprisingly, or perhaps not, I discover that the structural problem has been present since 1989. Why this has not been detected before amazes me.

I listen to the Stuart Hall ad on the radio and it sounds good.

Our opponents on Saturday, Yeovil Town, are the only team in the Conference, and even the league who, so far this season, are unbeaten away. And, with another 500 Viking helmets being given away, it should be a great day.

Wednesday 10 February

The cost of carrying out repairs to the popular stand will be £5,000 and there is no other option than to pay it, fans safety being our priority.

England play France at Wembley with a team chosen by caretaker manger Howard Wilkinson. England lose 2-0, Nicholas Anelka scoring both goals.

Thursday 11 February

Arrive late in the office, needing my early morning fix of coffee. Once again I have been delayed, due to an accident on the Stocksbridge by-pass, near Sheffield. The accident has occurred at an awkward position on the road network, causing me to take a very lengthy detour. Why can't accidents be more thoughtful, causing less inconvenience to us, already stressed-out, drivers?

February 1999

Good news, repairs on the stand should be completed today.

The afternoon is spent clearing paper work as I can't see over the top of my desk again.

Friday 12 February

A quick interview with Claire Dalton at Radio Sheffield, promoting the events we've planned for Saturday's game. The Viking helmets and Quid a Kid scheme have caught the media's attention.

At lunch time, I nip out to buy my wife a Valentine card and one for her birthday, being on the same day. Before choosing a Valentine card, men have to carefully consider the state of their relationship. Others may feel it's enough to have remembered the occasion. On buying cards to be sent by myself and the two kids, I shop for presents. I often ask Elise, what can I buy the woman who has everything? Her reply is not fit to print here. After buying wine glasses, wine and a box of chocolates, my mobile rings. I have to return to the Club, Kevin Phelan urgently requires some information to be faxed to him.

'Horny' (Photo by Paul Gilligan).

Saturday 13 February

We are 17th in the league. Let's hope today, with the match against Yeovil, we can take our unbeaten run to seven games and, inch further up the table, away from the relegation zone. I wonder though, if the two-week break will affect the team's confidence.

Eric Randerson and members of the Rovers Women's F.C. (Photo by Paul Gilligan).

All 500 Viking helmets are distributed both inside and outside the ground.

A crowd of 4,413 witnesses an abysmal performance by the referee, who sends off Mark Hume, only two minutes after coming on as a substitute. The referee also makes Ian Snodin spend the second half in the Directors' Box, following comments made at half-time.

We lose 2-0 and Yeovil were, by far, the better side, having Warren Patmore, a colossus of a player, up front, causing us all kinds of problems.

Albert Paget, tells me of two ugly incidents that occurred during the game. The referee was attacked as he left the field, so too was a Yeovil player. The referee informs me a plastic bottle was thrown on to the pitch.

There is no complaint, about any trouble, by the Yeovil directors afterwards in the Board Room, receiving congratulations for their team's performance.

Driving home, I consider the seriousness of this afternoon's incidents, as we are already on a warning from the FA, after the Dover pitch invasion. I fear the worst.

Fortunately, the referee did not see the remonstrations or the shouting of John Ryan against some of the decisions he made.

I will send a report to the FA about the referee's performance today, though they are, nearly always, ignored.

February 1999

Monday 15 February

During the morning, a behind closed doors game is played against Mansfield Town, Rovers winning 3-0, through a Matt Caudwell hat-trick. I feel this player will definitely be a star of the future, and will move for a substantial transfer fee.

A fax has been received from Barrow F.C. asking for support, in their fight to stay in the Conference. The Chairman and myself adhere to their request by sending a letter to the FA.

Kevin Keegan is talking to the FA and, expects to be offered the England job.

Sheffield United and Arsenal agree to replay their cup game following a controversial incident during the first encounter. Personally, I feel this is setting a dangerous precedent.

A 'phone call from a PFA official, informing me that a former Rovers player wants a loyalty bonus, arguing it was never paid to him. I submit that he is not entitled to one and, at the end of the conversation, I can't help but feeling astounded at the number of ploys players will use to earn more money. A weaker club might have paid up.

Tuesday 16 February

Another nightmare journey on the roads, being re-routed several times. I now know about 50 different ways of reaching Doncaster from Oldham.

The first team is playing another closed doors game away at Leeds United.

John Ryan, Dave Parker and myself agree the contents of a Press release, to be sent out, condemning the action of a few fans at the Yeovil game.

Copies of newspapers are received from Yeovil, reporting on the incidents which took place during last Saturday's match.

I nip out for an X-ray on one of my big toes, which is giving me some trouble. This is the legacy of once being a professional footballer, where operations and X-rays are part of everyday life.

I am interviewed again by the BBC about the progress we have made since the Richardson era.

Wednesday 17 February

Kevin Keegan has agreed to take the England job on a part-time basis whilst still continuing at Fulham. Eventually, it is predicted, he will take the England job full-time.

Chairman John Ryan speaks to Ian Snodin about the Club's disciplinary record, which is possibly the worst in the Conference. We will have to take care, because if it worsens, there could be a fine imposed or points deducted. We are, without doubt, not a 'dirty' team. We just seem to have been a little unlucky.

Thursday 18 February

A Conference meeting is being staged at Hednesford Town, where I am finally introduced to Ken Scott, whose company handle the Conference's PR. Details of the league's agreement with Nationwide are revealed, and Ken must take some of the credit for bringing this about.

Barrow F.C's situation is very precarious, liquidators now deciding how long they will remain in business. They could still be booted out of the Conference, even before the last game of the season. Clearly, there ought to be a better system.

Friday 19 February

Fog is my companion for most of the journey to Doncaster.

Sometimes it's not worth being away from the office for a day, as too much paper work accumulates in my absence.

Our cash flow is very tight, and I discuss with Paul May, holding off payments to creditors a little longer. They can wait another week.

I make an enquiry, to the chairman of another Conference club, about one of their players. He rudely asks me why would the player want to transfer to Doncaster of all places. In any event, he adds, I bet you can't afford him. I quickly bite my tongue and politely end the conversation. I didn't think his attitude befitted that of a football club chairman. I wonder how he will feel if we land the Endsleigh Trophy? That would make him eat his words.

Claire Dalton, at Radio Sheffield, interviews me about the crowd trouble at the Yeovil game. I adopt my best Richard Burton voice while explaining to her that we are doing all we can to ensure the situation does not arise again.

Saturday 20 February

On a very sunny day, John Ryan and myself are journeying towards Forest Green Rovers, a place we couldn't even locate on any map, eventually discovering the club is based near Nailsworth, Gloucestershire. In some ways, visiting the various Conference grounds this season has been like an expedition. Nevertheless, Forest Green are doing well as a Conference side.

We take a massive detour, avoiding traffic congestion on the M5, only to encounter further problems along country lanes, eventually arriving at 'The Lawn', home of Forest Green Rovers.

It's a poor game, on an awful pitch, resulting in a very boring 0-0 draw. Before leaving, we glance at the league tables on the teletext, showing that we are still in 17th position, though a little nearer safety.

Monday 22 February

Telephone conversation with Paul May about financial problems. No sooner have I replaced the receiver on its cradle than Peter Wetzel makes contact. He explains that as a result of Glynn's scouting trip to Scotland, John Ryan and himself are willing to finance a deal, bringing Raith Rovers' Marvin Andrews to Doncaster. Afterwards, I speak to their manager Jimmy Nicholl who, clearly, does not want this player to leave. But, we understand the chairman is keen to sell, because of the club's financial situation. I ask to speak to Marvin Andrews, though Jimmy Nicholl wavers and says he will speak to him first and then 'phone back. It's reminiscent of the times when I used to 'phone girlfriends to ask them for a date, only to encounter their mothers, saying they were out or were unable to come to the 'phone. And, invariably, the messages I left, were never passed on.

I stay the night in Doncaster.

Tuesday 23 February

I didn't have a good night's sleep due to my annual bout of tonsillitis. Being a coward, I will not have them removed. Tonight, I need to stay over again as there is a home game against Telford, though I'm told there are no rooms available at the Earl. I will have to get A. Jeffrey Jnr to sort something out.

My first call is to Jimmy Nicholl in Scotland, who informs me that Marvin Andrews does not want to come to Doncaster. In any event, Raith will not accept the price we have offered. I ask to speak to the player's agent. J. Nicholl says he will 'phone later with the details.

By 4 pm, J. Nicholl has not made contact, so I 'phone him. I'm told he is out for the rest of the day – shades of the 'girlfriend's mother' syndrome again.

It appears that Brazilian international, Rivaldo, has turned down an £18 m. move to Man. Utd. Maybe he will consider a move to Doncaster, if the Marvin Andrews deal falls through? ...

Suffering from tonsillitis, I feel progressively worse as the day goes on. I 'phone my wife to get some sympathy, receiving none from the female staff who claim that whenever I am ill everyone knows about it. Surely not!

Later, Rovers win Telford 2-1, taking the team to 15th position in the league, and closer to safety.

The editor (Peter Tuffrey) attends his first Rovers game in months, and is impressed with the team's overall performance. Additionally, he mentions his old chum, John Ryan, is still as loud and as demonstrative, during a match, as he always has been in the past, the new role of chairman not having a calming effect at all.

A late cancellation at the Earl, finds me safely installed there once more for the evening.

Wednesday 24 February

The early arrival of Paul May sees us both assessing the present financial situation and cash flow for the remainder of the season. It cannot be assumed that everything will be all right when John Ryan takes over, we have to operate on a day-to-day basis on the premise that a beneficiary is not waiting round the corner to help us out.

I arrive home after two days away, discovering that Connor left school early, feeling ill. Elise is unwell and has not been to work, while Nolan, well, he's just Nolan ...

Thursday 25 February

I telephone J. Nicholl, though I am told he will be out until early afternoon. I stress that it is important he replies as soon as possible.

A discussion with the commercial staff is organised, stressing that more funds need to be generated. Whilst doing a great job, they have to do even better to help us keep afloat.

In time, J. Nicholl makes contact, repeating his earlier statement that the player we're interested in does not want to come to Doncaster. I relay the message to Ian Snodin who says he only wants players who have a genuine desire to join the Club.

Friday 26 February

Spend some time considering how we will survive financially through the close season, May-August. As this Club operates on a 'full time' basis, we have to pay players all the year round, unlike most other Conference clubs who are part-time. Our wages may be lower than the others in the league yet, being full time, we have to pay National Insurance contributions, all this impacting on our meagre finances.

Saturday 27 February

Hereford at home today, making it a clash between two former Football League clubs.

Connor is with me for moral support.

Rovers have several key players missing: Colin Sutherland and Mark Hume, are suspended while T. Wright, Shaun Goodwin, and Jason Minett are all injured. This means there's a home debut for Matt Caudwell.

With ten minutes to go, we're winning 2-1 through two Ian Duerden goals, and a penalty is awarded. Everyone is expecting the ball to be handed to Duerden so that he can complete a hat-trick, though up steps skipper, Dave Penney, to take it. Of course this is the professional thing to do, and Penney scores, securing victory. A great crowd of 3,568 sees the Club climb to the dizzy heights of 14th in the table, with only one defeat so far this year.

On the way home, Connor insists that we stop for the obligatory McDonalds.

Monday 1st March

Agree to meet some Rovers fans, one of whom was ejected from the ground, earlier in the season, and subsequently barred. After a frank discussion with the individual, I say the restriction will be lifted, though any further trouble will result in a life ban. Everyone makes mistakes, and I feel it is prudent to give him another chance.

Today sees the launch of our after school programme, called Latch-key Kids, which will, hopefully, provide children with an opportunity to develop their football skills. I think it is sad indictment of the current education system that teachers are no longer able to provide a similar service after school.

Tuesday 2 March

Our full back, Simon Shaw, has been chosen for the England semi-professional team, playing

Italy tonight. The team is picked from players in the Conference and other leagues below this level. I am only disappointed that Simon is not joined by more Rovers players.

Northwich Victoria are the visitors tonight, playing us in the Quarter Final of the Endsleigh Cup. Before the kick-off, I speak to Ian Snodin, who believes it is a game we can win, given our current form. It would be a fairy tale end to the season if we could lift this trophy. We already know that, should we win tonight, our opponents in the next round will be Morecambe, a team we have beaten twice this season.

At the end of the evening, we are celebrating a well-deserved 3-2 victory, a score line which flatters Northwich.

Bring on Morecambe …

Wednesday 3 March

John Moules, who went to last night's England semi-pro game, tells me that Simon Shaw had a good outing in the team's 4-1 victory.

The Endsleigh Cup Semi-Final dates are agreed, with the first leg being played at Morecambe on 30 March.

There are rumours that a number of League clubs are interested in signing Ian Duerden and Simon Shaw. Ian Snodin, John Ryan and Paul May agree to offer the players two year contracts this week.

Thursday 4 March

Today, I'm wearing my commercial dept. hat, travelling to Pride Park, Derby County's ground, for a seminar and exhibition on merchandising. Whenever I attend this type of event, I always find it very stimulating. Arguably, the day's main attraction is a key note speech from Edward Freedman, the man behind the Man. Utd revolution and, more recently, the Spice Girls success. Representatives from his company are currently working alongside Italian and Spanish football clubs, trying to orchestrate similar commercial revolutions.

Many clubs, in both the Conference and the League, have not yet realised the importance of merchandising. Fortunately, Rovers chairman, John Ryan, is aware of its significance.

During the lunch break, a raffle is drawn and it's a surprise to learn I've won a bottle of whisky. Whilst collecting the prize, some joker shouts, that's all Donny will win this season. We shall see about that.

In the afternoon, I'm asked to host one of the discussion groups, and deliver a key note speech about Football PR/Marketing. It's reassuring to learn they feel someone from Doncaster Rovers has a worthwhile contribution to make.

My speech went down well and hopefully brought a smile to a few faces.

Personally, I was impressed by a presentation on a card system which fans may use at a football ground like a normal credit card. By using the 'club' card the fan indicates certain patterns of behaviour, the data from which can be assessed in detail, and used in a variety of ways.

Disgraced boss 'left in tatters'

Ex-Rovers chief 'a sorry figure' as he goes to jail

Afterwards, I make a number of contacts, and we exchange business cards. A tour round Pride Park reveals the ground is impressive, though not the best in the world. However, it would be more than welcome in Doncaster.

Friday 5 March

Catching up on office work.

Saturday 6 March

Early morning in Oldham and the ground is covered with snow. Nolan's face is a picture of excitement, gazing out of the window.

I arrive at John Ryan's house, discovering the snow has also brushed its way through Cheshire. We check to see if the Woking game is still on, the question surprising their officials as it's a beautiful sunny day down there.

We arrive at the ground about 1.30 pm, not anticipating the unfriendly reception we are

Piece from the Doncaster Star, 6 March 1999.

about to receive. It's an ordeal getting some complimentary tickets for our guests and, after leaving them with an official, we discover the Board Room is not ready for us. Consequently, we are shown into a bar area by an elderly gentleman who bemoans the fact that we've received 10 free tickets. Two minutes later, I am asked for assistance in getting our mascot and helper into the ground, as Woking officials won't let them in free.

March 1999

Once we've gained access to the Board Room, a woman almost has coronary when our President Alick Jeffrey Snr, fresh from his sabbatical in Tenerife, lights up a cigarette. She insists the Board Room is a non-smoking area.

We appear to be encountering every rule in the world …

It's a poor game and we lose 2-0. Afterwards, Ian Snodin is refused entry to the Board Room because he is wearing track suit. Enough is enough, the chairman and myself making a speedy exit.

Monday 8 March

Most of my day is taken up working out figures for a crucial meeting with John Ryan. I leave at 7.30 pm, hoping to lay out the information on a spread sheet at home. At 11pm, with most of the work completed, my PC crashes, the data irretrievable. I kick an imaginary dog.

Tuesday 9 March

Deep snow is nestling on 'the tops', and torrential rain greets me on arrival in Doncaster. A little later, I manage to successfully put the figures on to a spread sheet.

The heavy rain is threatening tonight's fixture which we are desperate to play, helping to balance the books. During the afternoon, a local referee, Ian Snodin and myself make a pitch inspection. After removing my goggles and snorkel, I reluctantly agree to call off the game.

A meeting with John Ryan, discussing the figures which, although I say it myself, are beautifully presented.

Contract offers are made to Ian Duerden and Simon Shaw and I believe the terms are favourable enough for them both to sign.

Wednesday 10 March

Speak to Ian Snodin who agrees that we cannot afford to run a reserve team next year, spending money, instead, on consolidating the first team.

Ian and Glynn are picking up Garforth Town player, Andy Watson, in Leeds and taking him over to John Ryan's Cheshire offices. The two brothers have been watching Andy for some time, and he's considering signing for us instead of Huddersfield Town or Middlesborough, who are both keen to have him on their books. John Ryan has agreed to pay his transfer fee and wages.

During the evening, I am told Andy has agreed to join us. I 'phone Paul May about the news. He tells me that, because of our serious cash flow difficulties, we cannot take this player until John Ryan transfers the asking price, of £25,000, into our account.

John Ryan agrees to do this and another piece of the jigsaw is completed.

Friday 12 March

I meet Andy Watson and the chairman of Garforth Town F.C., who turns out to be a Doncaster Rovers fan. We go through the formalities of Watson's transfer, and the player signs on the dotted line.

Simon Shaw is selected for the England semi-pro side against Holland.

Saturday 13 March

Andy Watson is introduced to 3,149 fans at our home game with Hayes. The Mayor of Doncaster, Yvonne Woodcock, is also a guest today. Frustratingly, we lose 1-0 and slip to 16th spot in the table, and relegation territory. As may have been predicted, Ian and Glynn are very upset at the defeat, and we agree not to speak any further, at this point, to Ian Duerden and Simon Shaw about their contracts. It is not the right time today.

New signing, Andy Watson (Photo by Shaun Flannery).

Monday 15 March

Monica Lewinsky is travelling round the country signing copies of her book and, today, visits Yorkshire. I hope my book is as popular as hers, but does not court the same notoriety.

During the morning, admission prices for next season are worked out and, a little later, I have lunch with Mike Davies from the *Don. Star*. We chat about Rovers' progress so far this season and I am delighted to hear he thinks our fortunes have been turned round and is excited about the future. We discuss the Endsleigh Cup and, in his own inimitable way he states: 'I think, Rovers will bloody win it.'

March 1999

We have come a long way this season, and it is nice when someone hands out a little praise. As for winning the cup, we shall have to see.

Mike invites me to a boxing evening on Thursday to meet several local businessmen. Whilst not a lover of the sport, I feel it will be worthwhile attending the event.

Tuesday 16 March

In a copy of Rovers fanzine, I am described as looking like Barry Evans on Eastenders. Whilst I don't watch the programme I will have to take a look to judge if this claim is true.

Tonight, we're playing Northwich Victoria away and I have decided to travel to the game on the team coach. Dunn-Line, the firm that provides the vehicles, sends one normally used by Derby County. This is luxurious and worth several hundred thousand pounds. I check to see if we are paying our normal rate, before relaxing in my leather recliner. This is definitely the way to travel.

At Nothwich, I bump into Peter Tunks and David McKnight, who live locally and wanted to come along and judge for themselves the progress we have made. I am also delighted to see Kevin Phelan and Dave Parker. Kevin is continuing negotiations over the stadium issues and Dave has brought his wife out for the night. What a strange thing to do!

At the end of an awful first half, there are no goals. The second half is much more entertaining and we are soon in front. However, I am concerned when there is a floodlight failure, which is eventually fixed, after what seems to be an eternity. With only a minute to go, we are 2-1 ahead, and awarded a penalty. Dave Penney picks up the ball, only this time hands it to Ian Duerden, who duly despatches it into the back of the net for his hat trick. We thoroughly deserve the victory, though Northwich did have two players sent off. While I'm in the Board Room, Ian Duerden informs me that the referee will not allow him to take the ball home, which is customary for the scorer of a hat trick. I speak to the Northwich directors, and they agree that I can buy the ball. I hand it to a delighted Ian Duerden, telling him jokingly that the cost will be deducted from his wages … But, I would gladly fork out for a ball each week if he scored a hat-trick.

Later, Kevin Phelan tells me that negotiations are progressing nicely with regard to building a new stadium for the Club. Taking that into account, it's been a good day.

Wednesday 17 March

I'm delighted to see that we are now lying 13th in the league. Meanwhile, there is a dog fight for top spot between Cheltenham, Rushden and Diamonds, and Kettering. The latter two teams played each other last night, the match ending in a draw. At this stage of the season, I fancy Rushden to finish in top position, only because Cheltenham are still involved in the Endsleigh and FA Cup trophies.

Thursday 18 March

I agree a deal with Jelly Belly where, at out next home game, they will supply 4,000 packets of jelly beans free of charge. I obtained these through a contact of Mike Davies'. Apparently, they are the best. It is just a bit of fun, though I am sure the kids (and adults) will enjoy them.

During the evening, I attend the boxing match with Mike Davies and friends, though the whole event is a blur as I've forgotten my spectacles.

Friday 19 March

My car is collected for a much-needed service.

I speak to the company who want to supply our kit next season. Unfortunately, they will not provide a training strip.

John Ryan is holidaying in South Africa though he still finds time to contact me for a chat about club affairs.

I'm having a good day until 4.15 pm when I am told that there is a major fault on my vehicle, and it cannot be returned today. I frantically rush around trying to organise a replacement.

Saturday 20 March

Andy Watson is on the bench for today's home game with Welling. When he eventually plays, I get a taste of his talents. With his first touch, he beats three players and shoots just inches over the bar. I am very impressed. Unbelievably, ten minutes later, he scores, in a comfortable 4-1 victory. I believe the crowd, numbering 2,952, have witnessed a remarkable talent in Andy Watson. I just hope everything works out well for him.

To many people outside the game, football players seem to have a glamorous life. Some do. The perks are great but, as with any job, there are many pit falls. I experienced one of these myself. From being on the verge of a lucrative transfer deal, I ended up never playing again. One day a player might be a football club's asset, the next, he could be on the scrap heap. I played my last game at 21, retiring about a year later. Fortunately, I had started part-time studies at a local college. Afterwards, I got a job with the police, but that, allegedly, was only because the Chief Inspector was a football fan. It has taken me 10 years to reach the position I currently hold. I have done this through sheer hard work, and funding from the PFA, gaining Post Graduate qualifications.

Ian and Glynn Snodin amongst the Jelly Beans (Photo from Sheffield Newspapers).

Ian Snodin and myself have implored our young players, such as Glen Kirkwood, Matt Caudwell and Andy Watson to consider their futures carefully, just in case things don't work out. We have suggested they might like to take advantage of the courses run by the PFA or even the local colleges.

The life of a professional footballer can be ended in a flash, either by injury or just being surplus to requirements. In short, all footballers setting out on their career need to be acutely aware of the ups and downs of the professional game.

Duerden in new deal for Rovers

Top striker signs two-year contract

Doncaster Star feature article, 24 March 1999.

Monday 22 March

Sadly, I hear that Steve Nicol is to leave, accepting an offer as a player/coach in the United States. This week's home game against Stevenage will be his last in a Rovers shirt. Whilst, I'm disappointed, there was clause in his contract, allowing him to leave if offered a coaching position.

Colin Sutherland has broken his wrist, meaning he may be out for the remainder of the season. The transfer deadline is on Thursday, so we need to sign a replacement for him as soon as possible.

A local fan is annoyed with a one-fingered salute from Tommy Wright, after he scored a goal. I have a word with Ian Snodin and he agrees to talk to the player about the incident.

I finalise the content of an advert, going out on the radio for Friday's Stevenage game. This will be played on Friday night due to a race meeting being held on the local racecourse, during Saturday afternoon.

Tuesday 23 March

Last night Cheltenham lost at Hednesford Town, making the Conference title race wide open.

I speak with John Ryan, holidaying in South Africa, and he tells me of his plans for next season.

During the evening, my attendance is required at a parent/teachers evening at Connor's school, where I'm told he is a model pupil. I ask if they are talking about my son. After this is confirmed, my wife and I, being very proud, agree to buy him a present in recognition of his good work.

At home, I peruse the teletext, learning that Rushden have beaten Leek, to go level with Cheltenham at the top. The promotion battle is hotting up, and the relegation scrap is equally as exciting at the foot of the table.

Wednesday 24 March

Ian Duerden signs his new contract, and Dave Parker is instructed to announce this via a Press release.

Conscious of the fact the transfer deadline is tomorrow, we are trying to sign a Leeds lad who is now playing in Scotland.

It appears that Rushden are desperately trying to sign Jamie Forrester, the Third Division's leading goal scorer, before the deadline. Presumably, this is to boost their promotion campaign.

At Belle Vue, I bump into Richard Haley, a local businessman, keen Rovers supporter, and once connected with the Save the Rovers campaign. I inform him that we may have to raise admission prices next season, gauging his reactions. He says we ought to maintain existing prices. I explain that the increase is to boost Ian Snodin's budget for players, and the Club's running costs. Once I have explained this, being a true fan, he agrees with the logic behind the increase.

Thursday 25 March

In accordance with the transfer deadline, we have managed to sign Martin Foster from Greenock Morton. Ian Snodin has never seen him play, but former Leeds United star Eddie Gray has urged us to sign him. So, due to the 5pm transfer dead line, we take a gamble.

In the afternoon, checks are made, ensuring everything is organised for tomorrow's home game with Stevenage.

At the end of the day, I talk with Ken Scott at the Conference, gleaning any news of transfer deals. Surprisingly, very little has taken place, even at Rushden or Cheltenham, who are pushing for promotion.

Friday 26 March

A meeting with commercial staff and Eric Randerson, going through the evening's activities, featuring music, fireworks, lots of give-aways and entertainment on the pitch before the game starts.

The afternoon is taken up with writing a proposal to John Ryan and Paul May for developing our own clothing label, producing players kit, replicas, and leisure wear.

The pre-match entertainment goes well, with jelly beans, wagon wheels and other items being distributed. I will accept no responsibility if kids throw up later.

Today, for the first time, the players will run on to the pitch to pop star Robbie Williams' record 'Let Me Entertain You,' and a firework display. Although Belle Vue is not the San Siro stadium, by any stretch of the imagination, we like to try and create an atmosphere.

Eric Randerson and his staff, distributing T-shirts and other merchandising items to the crowd, receive applause as they leave the field.

The crowd of 4,629, is the highest of the season. It includes about 100 from Stevenage, and everyone watches a very exciting game, though it ends 0-0.

Quite a number of adults are disappointed on not getting any free jelly beans or wagon wheels.

Steve Nicol receives a warm applause after his last game for Rovers, and a special presentation is made by Peter Wetzel and John Ryan. We wish him well.

Farewell to Steve Nicol (Photo by Paul Gilligan).

Monday 29 March

I'm feeling a little delicate this morning, heading over the tops, as both my sons were Christened yesterday and a small family celebration was held afterwards. The boys, Nolan and Connor, are three and six respectively, and I thought they were a little too old to undergo this ritual. But, my wife always gets her way in the end ...

A letter from the FA says they are taking no further action over the incidents at the Yeovil game. So, providing we keep out of trouble for twelve months, there should be no problems.

Tuesday 30 March

Today sees the first leg of the Endsleigh Cup Semi-Final at Morecambe (who are the holders) and once again I am travelling to the game on the team coach. As usual, Alick Jeffrey Jnr picks on journalist Peter Catt, who accompanies the team to all away games, though the banter is good-natured and relaxes the Snodin bothers.

At Morecambe, I meet up, once more, with Ian Green, Rovers original chairman at the outset of the season, and he's delighted to see that we have progressed thus far, in this competition.

Simon Shaw is away on England duty; Tommy Wright, and 'Dino' are injured. Kevin McIntyre is 'cup-tied' having played earlier in the campaign while on loan to Barrow. Something, he now regrets. Andy Watson and Martin Foster are in the starting line-up for the first time. As the game begins, Foster plays well and Watson continues to impress with his balance, speed, natural ability and skills, with both feet.

We are 2-0 up at half-time, Ian Duerden scoring both goals. The start of the second half sees Shaun Goodwin off with an injury, and Colin Sutherland, playing with a broken wrist, now has a shoulder injury. With 15 minutes to go, the referee is seemingly intent on letting Cup holders Morecambe back into the game. He sends off Jason Minett and awards two penalties in quick succession, against Rovers. Amazingly, our goalie, Andy Woods saves them both. Although Morecambe do score a late goal, over 500 Rovers fans go home happy.

I believe, we should at least reach the final and, who knows, maybe win the cup.

Wednesday 31 March

After last night's splendid victory, the phone is constantly ringing, with people showering congratulations on the team. However, we remind them that the job is still only half done.

A meeting is held with Emlyn Hughes' son, working as a rep for his father's merchandising company. I say a decision will be made about ordering some goods at a later date.

I must admit that I enjoyed watching the Liverpool team that included Emlyn Hughes. They played some incredible football and, on their day, were unbeatable. As a kid, I recall taking a radio with me to bed and listening under the blankets to their European Cup match against St Etienne. David Fairclough came on as substitute to score the winner.

Thursday 1 April

Meetings take up much of my time during the morning, not falling victim, thankfully, to any April Fool pranks.

John Ryan and Kevin Phelan are together at the Club and subsequently tell me that a date for the take-over is getting closer. It would be good to announce the details on a match day.

After consultation with John Ryan, we agree to manufacture our own kit/leisure wear. This is major step for the Club, and can be sustained by our large fan base. We will start work on designs very soon.

Saturday 3 April

I travel with John Ryan to our away match with Kidderminster Harriers, eventually finding the ground, in spite of the lack of road signs. Yet, Kidderminster have an impressive little ground.

In an exciting game, and with plenty of team spirit, Rovers draw 3-3. The only bad news is that our player, Shaun Goodwin, sustains a badly dislocated and broken finger.

Easter Monday 5 April

We're hoping for a good crowd at today's home game with Hednesford Town. As the match progresses we have about 20 shots, but can't score, their keeper making some incredible saves. They have one shot and take the lead, a crowd of 3,595 witnessing something which has happened too many times this season.

To make matters worse, there is a fault on our PA system, creating a safety problem. This will have to be repaired, incurring more cost, before next Thursday's match with Morecambe in the second leg Semi-Final of the Endsleigh Cup.

Tuesday 6 April

Invited to attend a radio chat show tomorrow, giving my opinions on sport in general. As it's live, I should be kept on my toes.

Wednesday 7 April

There's good news for me. My place on the players' end of season trip to Magaluf has been confirmed. The trip is to be funded by John Ryan. I will probably persuade him to write a note to my wife, asking her permission for me to attend.

John Ryan is in London today, having another meeting with the F.A., outlining details of the take-over, and the new stadium. Kevin Phelan tells me that we will certainly be able to make an announcement about the take-over before the end of the season.

Interestingly, I hear that the two other teams in the Endsleigh Cup Semi-Final, Farnborough and Cheltenham, have agreed to play only one of the two scheduled games, due to the fixture congestion on the part of Cheltenham. The two teams are playing this game tonight.

John Ryan makes contact, saying the F.A. meeting went well, and does not envisage any problems arising.

At 5.30 pm, I drive to Radio Leeds, for the chat show. When talking, I put on my best accent, but don't say 'claaass' or 'graaass', as is customary with most people on the BBC. I believe that it sounds awful when people try to 'improve' their accent.

A little later, I'm a guest at Garforth Town's annual dinner, arriving at about 8.45 just in time for the sweet course (or pudding, if you've not got a BBC voice). I was expecting to see Andy Watson, who we signed from Garforth a short time ago, only with a game tomorrow, I'm sure Ian Snodin has safely tucked him up in bed. I sit next to guest speaker Emlyn Hughes, and mention that I saw his son a few days ago. When it's his time to perform he does so in his typically honest, blunt, humorous, forthright way.

Instead of travelling home tonight, I'm staying in Doncaster at the Earl. There's a message on my mobile from Connor, saying he'd like a pair of new soccer boots, in recognition of him doing well at school. That perks me up and brings a smile to my face, though I do miss both boys.

On reaching the hotel, which is deserted except for Wesley the night porter, I have a coffee in the bar. A little later, I flick through the teletext, amazed to discover that Farnborough, already relegated from the Conference, have beaten Cheltenham 2-0. To my mind, this means we have a great chance of lifting the cup.

Thursday 8 April

An early morning call from Emlyn Hughes Snr, who wants to know if we would like to order any of his stock. I politely answer that when we are ready to do so, I will be in touch.

Much of the morning is taken designing logos, and playing/training kits for John Ryan's approval.

Around the town, hopes are high for us to beat Endsleigh Cup holders, Morecambe, in tonight's Semi Final game.

A crowd of 3,297 watch a dour contest, the two teams separated at full time by an Andy Watson goal, sending Rovers into their first senior cup final for years.

Who would have guessed, all those months ago, we would be in this position? I cannot express the satisfaction it gives me. Yes, we would love to win the cup, and have a great chance of doing it.

I stay over, having a few beers with Ian Snodin and Alick Jeffrey Jnr, and the following conversation takes place.

A.J. Jnr: 'When we play the second leg at Belle Vue, the ground will be full.'
I.S.: 'I think at least 5,000-6,000 will be there.'
I.M.: 'Do you think so?'
A.Jnr: 'As people were leaving the ground tonight, they were talking about how many will come to the final.'
I.M.: 'It's an incredible achievement.'
I.S.: 'We have certainly come a long way.'
A.Jnr: 'Cheers' (lifting his glass).
I.M.: 'Hey, do we have a trophy cabinet?'
A.J.jnr: 'I don't think so.'
I.S.: 'We'd better get one made, because we're going to win this cup.'

Friday 9 April

After the win last night, a buoyant atmosphere permeates throughout the Club. I speak to representatives at the Conference, congratulating us on reaching the final. I point out that it would be wise to play the second leg of the final in Doncaster. A crowd of around 5,000 might be anticipated, being financially beneficial to all concerned – the Conference taking 25% of the proceeds, thus swelling their coffers.

I use the remainder of the day to complete a number of reports, finishing early at 4 pm to go home to the ball-and-chain, and the kids. Connor regurgitates all the information, about last night's game, gleaned from the teletext.

Saturday 10 April

Rovers have no game today, so I'm drafted in to play for Oldham rugby union veterans, in a tough encounter with Huddersfield YMCA. I use the game as a safety valve, letting off steam because, of late, I've kicked the imaginary dog, too often.

In my customary full-back position, my friend Chubby says I'm slower than I look – a phrase often heard during my playing career.

During the evening, I attend a house-warming party, bumping into John Ryan. I hope no one bumps into me, as my body still aches from the game earlier on.

Monday 12 April

On arrival at the Club, I learn that Doncaster Dragons have sacked their coach, after only holding the position for a few weeks. Given time, I'm sure the rugby club can be turned round. And, it's a shame Westferry are not involved.

A sportsman's dinner is organised for this evening, where Gordon Banks – one of my all-time heroes – is the guest speaker. When I was five years old, I remember him making that superb save against Pele in the 1970 World Cup. In my short career, I've probably seen better saves, though none more important than that one.

I'm taking John Ryan's place on the top table this evening as he is unable to attend. When the function begins, with about 200 people in attendance, there's no sign of our guest speaker, though I'm not panicking, just yet. Many speakers have a habit of not appearing until after the meal. However, I send out Alick Jeffrey Jnr to try and make contact with Gordon Banks. He returns to say this is proving futile. And, the goalkeeping legend does not show. I tell Alick and Nigel I will speak to them about this in the morning.

Fortunately, Alick is a very good friend of local raconteur, John (son of Nobby) Stiles, a former Doncaster Rovers and Leeds United player, who agrees to stand in and spout some of his own footballing tales. His performance, alongside that of Master of Ceremonies Malcolm Lord, deflect from what, otherwise, might have a disastrous evening.

Comedian Paddy Green was hilarious, his act including the following gag: 'Mary and Joseph go to an inn at Christmas, asking the landlord, any rooms for the night? The landlord says, no we're full. Joseph says, yeah sorry, I forgot it's Christmas.'

Tuesday 13 April

The first job is to get Nigel and Alick into my office and ask them why Gordon Banks did not show. It transpires that he had been waiting outside the Belle Vue offices from 7.30 pm until 9 pm. No contact numbers were left with him, nor with Nigel or Alick. He was not informed of the venue, though contact was hindered by the fact that, until yesterday, he was away in Spain for a month. The whole incident illustrated a serious communication breakdown, for which Nigel and Alick receive a bollocking. Nevertheless, it was the most successful sportsman's evening so far, and I compliment them both on this fact. I doubt if the two will make the same mistakes again, judging by the leg-pulling they receive afterwards from the Snodins.

Later, Nigel, Alick and myself discuss the forthcoming Endsleigh Cup final, and we decide to make it a spectacular evening, with a full programme of pre-match entertainment, including fireworks and give-aways.

I put the finishing touches to a kit design, which harks back to the 1960s. I'm hoping to finalise a deal next week with the manufacturer. We need to launch the kit during the summer.

Snow has caused problems at some cricket games, which just about sums up British weather.

During the evening, I check on the results from the Conference games. Cheltenham have won, taking a five point lead at the top. Rushden lose at home to Yeovil, and Leek's game was called off. Farnborough, already relegated, look like being joined by either Leek or Barrow. Yesterday, Leek sacked their manager.

Extract from the Doncaster Star.

Tuesday 14 April

On studying the Conference table this morning, I note that taking three points from tonight's game with Northwich ought to make us safe from relegation.

John Ryan and Peter Wetzel are talking with Ian and Glynn about the various budgets for next year. The two brothers need to know, as soon as possible, the finance available. This will also determine the players to be kept and those to be released. They want to disclose this information soon after the second leg of the Endsleigh Final. This is the reality of football. No one's future is assured. One day a player can be holding a cup winners medal, the next, looking for a new club.

A bitterly cold night attracts a crowd of 2,296, witnessing a disappointing 2-2 draw, though we inch our way to safety.

I stay the night in Doncaster, catching the highlights of the Man. United/Arsenal cup replay. Ryan Giggs' winner in extra time will be talked about for a long time ahead.

April 1999

Wednesday 15 April

I pencil in the names of people to be included on the end of season tour. Ian Snodin and myself agree that those players, released by the Club, will not be invited. I discover that a pre-arranged personal visit to Dublin clashes with the Club's trip, therefore I will join everyone two days late.

A pre-season friendly is arranged with Leeds United. This match will also act as a fitting tribute to Steve Beaglehole, a former youth coach at Doncaster and now with Leeds.

Albert Paget tells me we have problems in a small area of the ground, which I will have to look into before the cup final.

Thursday 16 April

Snow has closed off many roads near where I live, with local authority 'gritting' teams working overtime. I ask the age old question: How do the drivers of the 'gritting' lorries get to work?

Fearful of another car crash, I drive slowly, trying to find a suitably safe route out of Lancashire. As may have been predicted, there is no snow in Doncaster.

I open an interesting letter from the PFA, asking the Club to co-operate with a company promoting a data-base, originally conceived by myself. The data-base tracks the progress of past and present players. Information accumulated is used in a variety of ways, supplementing the already outstanding work of the organisation.

I have decided not to travel to Farnborough for tomorrow's game, but will go there next Tuesday, when we play them again in the first leg of the Endsleigh Final.

Saturday 17 April

At around 6pm, I speak to Ian Snodin about the 1-0 defeat we have suffered. Whilst Ian is devastated by the result, he did leave out six key players, saving them for the Final, though it has proved today, Farnborough will be no push over.

The defeat is somewhat softened when we learn that the teams below us have also lost, making us safe from relegation, news we have wanted to hear all season. Whilst most people won't regard staying in the Conference as an achievement, it means a lot to us, after all we have endured. We have managed to survive the most traumatic season in the Club's history. From now on, the only way is up. During the evening, I go out, celebrating with my wife and children.

Monday 19 April

I'm still sore after playing rugby on Saturday for the Oldham Vets against The Rags, made up from different clubs in Yorkshire – a real war of the roses. It seemed a good idea at the time, only I'm having second thoughts now.

John Ryan informs me that he has finalised all the details for the Magaluf trip – including written permission from my wife.

In the afternoon, students from Doncaster College interview me as part of a video project they are producing about the Club. Let's hope it ends on a happy note, with us lifting the Endsleigh trophy.

April 1999

During the evening, I'm a guest of Doncaster Schools, presenting the trophy at the under-19s Final.

Duties for the day completed, I arrive home at 10 pm.

Tuesday 20 April

Good news. Ian Snodin has offered Colin Sutherland a new contract. Since Christmas he has displayed outstanding form.

12.30 pm and I'm on the team bus, setting off for Farnborough. Soon afterwards, the card school begins. Unfortunately for journalist Peter Catt, physiotherapist John Bowden and Ian Snodin, I'm making up the fourth member of the school today.

We have the obligatory pre-match meal, before travelling to the ground. I help to carry in the 'skips' containing the kit, and hear that John Bowden has a request. He wants to be left alone to put out the kit. Football is full of superstitions and however bizarre they might be, are nearly always respected. Therefore, John is left alone …

Meanwhile, Ian, Glynn, Alick and myself inspect the pitch, noticing pools of surface water after torrential rain. In what can only described as a token gesture to rectify the problem, the groundsman uses a sponge to mop them up.

'Don't worry, they will be gone in half-an-hour,' he quips optimistically.

We head back to the hotel to pick up the players, returning soon afterwards.

John Ryan joins us from his London office, mentioning that the take-over will be finalised tomorrow.

Surprisingly, there's a poor crowd of 630, with at least 300 from Doncaster, who witness the team emerge 1-0 victors of the first leg, through a Dave Penney goal. It was not a great performance by us, but who cares in a cup final? This now sets the scene for a great match in the remaining leg at Belle Vue.

There's a relaxed atmosphere on the way back, to such an extent that I'm allowed to re-join the card school. Whilst we've won the first leg of the final, everybody's feet are still firmly on the ground.

'We haven't won anything yet,' says Ian Snodin.

He puts on one of his favourite tapes, which is met with grunts and groans from the players. They want to hear something like an Ibiza anthem, and I'm with them on that. However, Ian pulls rank, playing the Drifters' greatest hits.

Members of the card school try to estimate how many fans will turn up to watch the return leg at Belle Vue. Alick predicts 5,000 and I don't think that figure is too optimistic.

We arrive back at 2 am, and I stumble into bed an hour later.

Wednesday 21 April

As might have been predicted, I'm bleary-eyed this morning, and everyone in the office wants to know details about last night's game. They predict the return leg will be a sell out, but we will have to keep quiet about that or the police will insist on it being 'all-ticket'.

April 1999

The commercial staff and myself get our heads together, planning the players' end of season awards, to be staged at the Earl. Ian and Glynn Snodin join us to decide the number of awards to be allocated.

On a separate issue, we agree that free admission will be given to children at our last home league game. This will serve as a fitting tribute to the fans, who have been tremendous throughout the season. It will also help them save money to attend the final, which is only a few days later. An announcement about kids attending free, will be made in the *Don. Star*.

In their evening match against Juventus, Man. Utd. make an amazing comeback, taking them to the European Cup Final. This is great news for English football.

Thursday 22 April

I hold a staff meeting at 10 am, having the unenviable task of telling them the Endsleigh Final is on a Bank Holiday Monday and they will have to work from 9 am until 10 pm. As we're short staffed, there's no other option, and breaks will have to be taken whenever possible. A number of volunteers are be drafted in, though I'm sure the staff will cope, being well organised in all their duties.

Friday 23 April

Throughout the day, I'm working on various preparations for the final. I've also been given the task of adjudicating on the players' annual awards.

Saturday 24 April

Today, we play our last away game of the season at Telford. There's nothing to compete for in terms of relegation issues, so it should be quite a relaxing game for everyone. Over 1,000 Rovers fans make the trip, and the kick-off has to be delayed 15 minutes for them all to be accommodated. Without doubt, they are perhaps the most loyal fans in the Conference. And, I think it proves that they are fully behind the Club, and that the awful events of the last few seasons are now behind us.

In a very one-sided game, we win 2-0, all our team members eager to impress and earn themselves a place in the cup final side.

Monday 26 April

An early call from John Shires, a presenter at Yorkshire Television, and I agree a deal with him. YTV will film the final and, from the footage, make a video, for us to sell. I act positively, firmly believing we can win the second leg, and order 1,000 copies. If we lose, kids may be able to use the videos as building blocks.

The video idea was put forward by Dave Parker, who has done much this season to keep us in the glare of the media spotlight.

Everything is being prepared for Wednesday evening's players' awards function at the Earl. Over 220 people are expected to attend, including players, their partners, and a number of sponsors. Names of players to receive a trophy have been submitted to the engraver and I am

April 1999

pleased to learn that Glynn Snodin will be recognised as the Club's worst dressed person. This will be presented tongue-in-cheek. I have to confess that I am lucky not to win the award myself.

John Ryan phones from Ireland.

J.R.: 'You may be delighted to hear that the deal has been completed and, from the first of May, Peter Wetzel and myself will be the new owners of Doncaster Rovers'.

Rovers get new men at the helm

Westferry agree deal

By Steve Hossack

CHAIRMAN John Ryan and wealthy businessman, Peter Wetzel, will take over the reins of Doncaster Rovers prior to Monday's Endsleigh Trophy final second leg against Farnborough at Belle Vue.

Mr Ryan announced at last night's inaugural awards dinner at the Earl of Doncaster, that the two men had struck a deal with Westferry Limited to acquire control of the Nationwide Conference League club.

"Westferry have done a great job since buying the club from the previous regime," he said.

"But it is a new start for the club which will now be owned by Doncastrians and Doncaster Rovers' supporters. We have ambitions and we have the money to back up our plans."

Mr Ryan said that both he and Mr Wetzel were determined to get the club back into the Football League and said that their ambitions didn't end there.

"When I first started watching the club 40 years ago, they were in the Second Division. I would love to see us back at that level, which is now the First Division."

He reflected on the sad scenes at the club's final Division Three game of the season against Colchester at Belle Vue last May and the genuine concerns for the club's future.

Amazing

He said it was amazing what progress had been made over the last 12 months.

"It has been a fantastic season," he told the packed gathering.

"We might not have won the Nationwide Conference League, but we have seen some great games. We have also managed to put a smile back on people's faces.

"The games against Dover at Belle Vue, when we came from 3-1 down to beat them 5-4, and the win at Rushden and Diamonds were the two highlights for me. As was the day we made Alick Jeffrey, who was a boyhood idol of mine, honorary club president."

Rovers' boss Ian Snodin paid tribute to brother Glynn, who he described as his "most important signing" of the season.

"He takes charge of all the training sessions and does a great job. All the lads enjoy the sessions even though he works them hard."

Both Snodin and Mr Ryan praised the loyalty of the fans.

Prize time: Chairman John Ryan presents the players' player of the year award to Lee Warren. Full report: p69.

Doncaster Star headline, 29 April 1999.

151

April/May 1999

I.M.: 'That's great news John.'

J.R.: 'We will put substantial funds into the Club. I want us to get out of the Conference and back into the Football League, where we belong, as soon as possible.'

I.M.: 'I hope that I can be part of it.'

J.R.: 'I want you to carry on doing the same job. And, I will ask Paul May to stay. We need some continuity at the club.'

We can now announce this news publicly.

Wednesday 28 April

A great atmosphere prevails at the Rovers players' awards dinner, the first one for many years. Well-known comedian and ex-Rovers player, Charlie Williams, presents a merit award to Simon Shaw, in recognition of him playing for the England semi-pro team. There are two jokey awards. Glynn Snodin takes the award for worst-dressed person in the spirit in which it was intended, and Glenn Kirkwood is handed the 'Yellow Jersey' award. Football is full of strange customs and this accolade is one of them, being given to the player who consistently under performs – in a fun way – during training. In fact, a player might be as skilful as Pele, yet still win the award.

The young player of the year is Ian Duerden, the Club's leading goal scorer. Lee Warren, who has been with the Rovers for five years, lifts the player's player of the year trophy. *Doncaster Star* has promoted this evening's event and, through a readers' poll, selects Colin Sutherland as the Rovers' player of the year. He celebrates in characteristic style, indicating why he is a favourite amongst team-mates and fans alike.

A late night is had by all, even Mike Davies from the *Don. Star* manages to buy me a shandy.

Thursday 29 April

There is extensive coverage of last night's event in this evening's *Don. Star*, many pictures shown in full colour. It is perhaps a remarkable indication of how things have been turned round at the Club.

Friday 30 April

A drive to Paul May's offices, agreeing a format for the smooth hand over of the Club to John Ryan and Peter Wetzel.

I need to return home by 7.15 pm, allowing my wife to leave for an appointment. Several routes are attempted to avoid traffic, before finally discovering one via Buxton, arriving home at 7.12 pm.

Saturday 1 May

Ian Snodin has left out five key players for today's home game with Kingstonian, although two of these have been enforced on compassionate grounds. Shaun Goodwin's father has been taken into hospital, and Andy Watson's grandmother died earlier this morning.

A better than expected crowd of 2,900 watch a poor game with Kingstonian, who win 1-0. There is talk after the game of over 5,000 coming to the final on Monday.

Monday 3 May

Due to anxiety, I'm unable to sleep, rising at 5 am. A little later, I decide to get ready and travel to Doncaster. Even though everything is organised for tonight's game, I double check, and make sure that staff are fully aware of their duties. Stadium manager Albert Paget tells me to relax, everything is under control and assures me there will be no problems.

There is a race meeting on the town's course today where John Ryan has hired one of the private boxes. I nip over to see him and say hello to his guests, desperately trying to fill in my time.

At 5.30 pm people are milling around outside the ground, and the shop has been doing a roaring trade all day. As kick-off time approaches, jelly beans are distributed once more and, this time, I have ordered twice as many as were handed out at the last home game.

The only bad news is that the sound system was sabotaged after the rugby game, yesterday. I desperately try to arrange for it to be fixed.

Peter Wetzel and John Ryan announce the new take-over to the fans
(Photo by Shaun Flannery).

John Ryan and Peter Wetzel are to appear on the pitch and announce details of the take-over before the start of game, which has to be delayed 15 minutes due to congestion outside the ground. When the announcement is eventually heard, it is greeted with a rapturous applause. John Ryan adds that the Club is now in the hands of people who are 'genuine Rovers fans.'

I have a brief conversation with two representatives from the Conference who are amazed at the size of the crowd, peaking at 7,160. Only about 100 fans have travelled from Farnborough. As the teams emerge on to the pitch, Robbie Williams' 'Let me entertain you,' blasts from the PA system, now repaired.

Player of the year, Colin Sutherland scores after five minutes and it looks as if the tie is over. Two more goals, scored by Duerden, sees Rovers comfortable winners.

Just before the end of the game, Ken Avis the MC, had asked fans to not run on the pitch. At the final whistle, over 4,000 people disobeyed the instruction.

In a scene that can only be described as my proudest moment in sport, Dave Penney hosts the Endsleigh Trophy to the cheer of over 7,000 people. I'm not renowned for showing my emotions in public, but this definitely brings a lump to my throat. Some people are actually crying tears of joy.

John Moules from the Conference asks me to pass on his congratulations to everyone at the Club. He is amazed at how we have coped with the large crowd – a record for an Endsleigh final.

I make for the changing rooms, congratulating the players, before being interviewed on television. The office staff are celebrating with a bottle of wine and, after such a win and working a 13-hour day, who can blame them?

Dave Penney leads the team out
(Photo by Malcolm Billingham).

Dave Penney lifts the trophy
(Photo by Malcolm Billingham).

When all the fans have gone, I wander out on to the pitch, chatting with Paul May.

I.M.: 'Well done Paul, we wouldn't have made it through the season without your help.'

P.M.: 'Yes, we have come a long way from those meetings in Brighouse.'

Later that evening, Ian Snodin, Alick, several others and myself have a few drinks in the bar at the Earl.

At some point during the evening, Ian Snodin and myself are alone together for a couple of minutes.

I.M.: 'I think you and Glynn have done a fantastic job this season. Staying in the Conference was always going to be a massive challenge, but to win a trophy in front of a full house, is absolutely incredible. It's the best day in football I've ever had.'

I.S.: 'Our fans are amongst the best in the world. After all the shit they've had to put up with, I'm glad we've achieved something for them. I was almost in tears at the end.'

I.M.: 'I'm not known for being emotional myself, but it was difficult not to be overcome by the event. A lot of people associated with the Club have worked hard this season, Paul May in particular. And, it's a time like this Ian, when you realise that all the scouting trips you been on and all the games you've watched, have all been worthwhile.'

I.S.: 'I know. The worst times were driving two hours to watch a player, then realising after ten minutes, he was crap, and starting the long journey home.'

I.M.: 'This season has been like a fairy tale.'

I.S.: 'Yeah, and there was over 7,000 in the ground tonight to see a happy ending.'

A.Jnr (on returning from the lavatory): 'If we're top of the table early next season, the ground will be full at every home game.'

I.S.: 'What do you know about football?'

A.J. Jnr: 'You've only won a cup, don't get too excited,' he then laughs.

As everyone drifts away, the Endsleigh Cup is left with me. I take it up to my room, staring at it for a while, the pressures of the season draining from me.

The only way is up.

Absolutely!

Ian Snodin sighs with relief on winning the Endsleigh trophy (Photo by Malcolm Billingham).

Rovers fans invade the pitch during the celebrations (Photo by Malcolm Billingham).

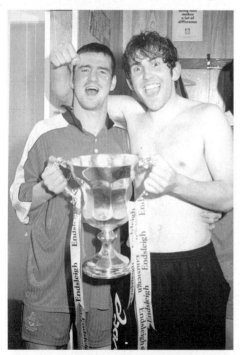

Colin Sutherland and Ian Duerden with the cup (Photo by Paul Gilligan).

Asda store (Bawtry Road) manager Peter Brigden holds the cup with Ian Snodin. Alick Jeffrey Jnr is in the background.(Photo by Paul Gilligan).

*Colin Sutherland, Ian Duerden, and Andy Watson celebrate with the fans
(Photo by Malcolm Billingham).*

Glyn Snodin leads the team celebrations (Photo by Shaun Flannery).

Nationwide
FOOTBALL CONFERENCE

Issue Number 38
4 May 1999

News release

- 6 MAY 1999

Reference: Doncaster Rovers

Rovers lift first cup honour

Doncaster Rovers are the 1999 winners of the Endsleigh Challenge Trophy. Ian Snodin's side lifted the **Nationwide Conference** honour with a 4-0 aggregate success over Farnborough Town, sealing the trophy with Bank Holiday Monday's 3-0 second leg victory over the Hampshire side. Goals from Ian Duerden (2) and Colin Sutherland earned Doncaster their first major cup success and their first piece of silverware since 1969 when they won the Fourth Division championship.

Monday's Endsleigh Trophy Final not only established a new record for the Belle Vue outfit, the 7,160 crowd attending the second leg is the highest ever recorded in the **Nationwide Conference** cup competition.

Extract from Conference News.

*Civic reception at the Mansion House with the Lady Mayor Yvonne Woodcock
(Photo from Sheffield Newspapers).*

NATIONWIDE CONFERENCE TABLE 1998-99

No	Club	P	W	D	L	Goals For	Ag	W	D	L	Goals For	Ag	Pts
1	Cheltenham Town	42	11	9	1	35	14	11	5	5	36	22	80
2	Kettering Town	42	11	5	5	31	16	11	5	5	27	21	76
3	Hayes	42	12	3	6	34	25	10	5	6	29	25	74
4	Rushden &Diamonds	42	11	4	6	41	22	9	8	4	30	20	72
5	Yeovil Town	42	8	4	9	35	32	12	7	2	33	22	71
6	Stevenage Borough	42	9	9	3	37	23	8	8	5	25	22	68
7	Northwich Victoria	42	11	3	7	29	21	8	6	7	31	30	66
8	Kingstonian	42	9	7	5	25	19	8	6	7	25	30	64
9	Woking	42	9	5	7	27	20	9	4	8	24	25	63
10	Hednesford Town	42	9	8	4	30	24	6	8	7	19	20	61
11	Dover Athletic	42	7	9	5	27	21	8	4	9	27	27	58
12	Forest Green Rovers	42	9	5	7	28	22	6	8	7	27	28	58
13	Hereford United	42	9	5	7	25	17	6	5	10	24	29	55
14	Morecambe	42	9	5	7	31	29	6	3	12	29	47	53
15	Kidderminster Harriers	42	9	4	8	32	22	5	5	11	24	30	51
16	Doncaster Rovers	42	7	5	9	26	26	5	7	9	25	29	48
17	Telford United	42	7	8	6	24	24	3	8	10	20	36	46
18	Southport	42	6	9	6	29	28	4	6	11	18	31	45
19	Barrow	42	7	5	9	17	23	4	5	12	23	40	43
20	Welling United	42	4	7	10	18	30	5	7	9	26	35	41
21	Leek Town	42	5	5	11	34	42	3	3	15	14	34	32
22	Farnborough Town	42	6	5	10	29	48	1	6	14	12	41	32

Final League table 1998-1999.

NATIONWIDE CONFERENCE
END OF SEASON STATISTICS 1998-99

	Attendances by Club Aggregate 1998-99	Average 1998-99	Average 1997-98	% Change
Barrow	34,108	1,624	1,325	+22.6
Cheltenham Town	65,354	3,112	1,837	+69.4
Doncaster Rovers	70,979	3,380	1,715	+97.1
Dover Athletic	22,750	1,083	1,069	+1.3
Farnborough Town	16,513	786	816	-3.7
Forest Green Rovers	17,925	854	697	+22.5
Hayes	15,967	760	661	+15.0
Hednesford Town	22,852	1,088	1,418	-23.3
Hereford United	41,494	1,976	2,477	-20.2
Kettering Town	42,700	2,033	1,491	+36.4
Kidderminster Harriers	40,823	1,944	2,023	-3.9
Kingstonian	27,307	1,300	700	+85.7
Leek Town	12,747	607	782	-22.4
Morecambe	24,425	1,163	1,532	-24.1
Northwich Victoria	23,949	1,140	1,101	+3.5
Rushden & Diamonds	63,924	3,044	2,552	+19.3
Southport	24,320	1,158	1,055	+9.8
Stevenage Borough	53,581	2,551	2,252	+13.3
Telford United	18,023	858	799	+7.4
Welling United	14,316	682	709	-3.8
Woking	46,942	2,235	2,801	-20.2
Yeovil Town	50,519	2,406	2,457	-2.0
Conference Total	**751,518**	**1,627**	**1,476**	**+10.23**

Conference clubs' attendance figures.

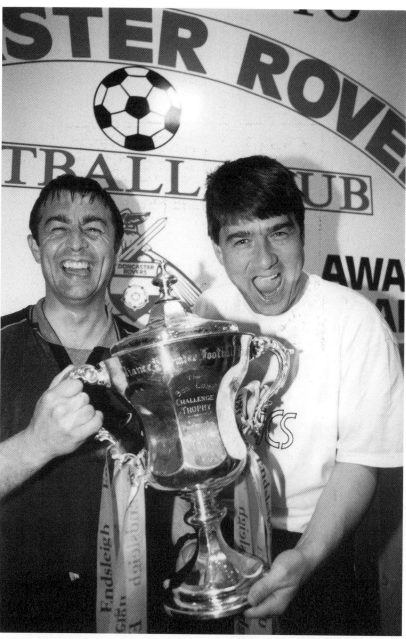

'Who would have thought, all those months ago, we would win this?'
(Photo by Malcolm Billingham).